High School Graduation

High School Graduation

K–12 Strategies That Work

Avis Glaze

Ruth Mattingley

Rob Andrews

Foreword by Ben Levin

A Joint Publication

CORWIN
A SAGE Company

FOR INFORMATION:

Corwin
A SAGE Company
2455 Teller Road
Thousand Oaks, California 91320
(800) 233-9936
www.corwin.com

SAGE Publications Ltd.
1 Oliver's Yard
55 City Road
London EC1Y 1SP
United Kingdom

SAGE Publications India Pvt. Ltd.
B 1/I 1 Mohan Cooperative Industrial Area
Mathura Road, New Delhi 110 044
India

SAGE Publications Asia-Pacific Pte. Ltd.
3 Church Street
#10-04 Samsung Hub
Singapore 049483

Acquisitions Editor: Arnis Burvikovs
Associate Editor: Desirée A. Bartlett
Editorial Assistant: Mayan White
Permissions Editor: Jennifer Barron
Project Editor: Veronica Stapleton Hooper
Copy Editor: Matthew Connor Sullivan
Typesetter: C&M Digitals (P) Ltd.
Proofreader: Wendy Jo Dymond
Indexer: Molly Hall
Cover Designer: Michael Dubowe

Copyright © 2013 by Corwin

Printed in the United States of America.

A catalog record of this book is available from the Library of Congress.

ISBN: 9781452217642

This book is printed on acid-free paper.

Certified Chain of Custody
Promoting Sustainable Forestry
www.sfiprogram.org
SFI-01268

SFI label applies to text stock

13 14 15 16 17 10 9 8 7 6 5 4 3 2 1

Contents

Lists of Tables, Figures, and Appendices

Foreword

The provision of public education to all children is one of the remarkable achievements of humanity. As recently as 50 years ago, the idea that virtually all young people could and should complete a secondary education would have been considered a dream, or wildly unrealistic. Even in "rich" countries, it is only recently that high school graduation has been seen as something that everyone should attain.

Today, across the globe, there is consensus on this issue. Political leaders campaign on it. College and university presidents want students with highly developed analytical and learning skills. Employers recognize that the economy depends on highly educated citizens when they ask for specific employability skills to address the demands of the workplace. Parents want their children to have the advantages conferred by more education, and students understand how important high school completion is for their futures. All stakeholders want schools to achieve higher levels of student success and graduation while, at the same time, helping students to develop personal, social, and interpersonal skills along with character attributes such as respect, responsibility, empathy, and fairness. And yet, in school systems everywhere, many students are not as successful as they can be.

While much of the rhetoric about education revolves around the idea that the competitiveness of a nation depends on the skills of its citizens and their ability to continue learning throughout their lives, that is only one aspect of the importance of education. Students also need to be attuned to the needs of their world and their local communities as they engage in community service and volunteerism. Education is recognized as vital to social cohesion and societies that are tolerant and caring. More than ever, there is a sense of urgency in achieving these outcomes as education is increasingly recognized as a driving force for societal improvement.

Educators everywhere are well aware of the mandate to realize both excellence and equity in student achievement. They are removing barriers to student success and ensuring that schools work to address the diverse needs of current student populations. Much has been accomplished, but there is much more to do. Students' backgrounds still play too large a role in shaping their futures, when what is wanted is a world in which outcomes are determined by effort and ability, and, more importantly, by the intervention strategies of the school, rather than accident of birth.

To realize this goal will require a coordinated effort and shared responsibility among all partners. Educators understand that high graduation rates benefit from a strong foundation that is established in the early years of a child's education. Engaging students and instilling a passion for learning begins in the early grades. As well, ensuring that there are intervention strategies for those who are not succeeding is needed at all grade levels. The sooner we begin, the greater the likelihood of rescuing those who need our support. At the same time, more and more evidence shows that people can turn around their lives at any point, and it is never too late for a student to move onto a better path and achieve success. No educator should accept the idea that if students have not been successful at some given point, the door is closed for good. Schools must be relentless in helping students achieve success, whatever their past.

High School Graduation: K–12 Strategies That Work validates the work that teachers, principals, systems leaders, and other educators have been doing in Ontario, across Canada, and around the world. Educators deserve gratitude, commendation, and encouragement for what they have already achieved in improving student achievement and narrowing achievement gaps. Ontario has increased its high school graduation rate by more than 20%, along with improving in literacy and numeracy skills of students in elementary schools, because of carefully designed and implemented improvement strategies. The lessons learned are powerful and consistent with other research on what it takes to bring about lasting system improvement.

One of the three goals of education in Ontario is to build public confidence in the education system. Public attitudes towards education have improved in the last nine years, and educator morale also improved significantly. The emphasis on helping educators improve their skills has been critical and will last for a long time. Schools will thrive when educators feel that there is no turning back and that they need to continue to build their knowledge of what works to improve achievement. The public, which sends its children to schools and pays the bills, deserves no less.

This book provides a comprehensive overview of the strategies that were used to improve education in Ontario. One important message is that success is dependent on a whole system approach at the district, school, and classroom levels. Schools cannot achieve the desired results alone. It takes a coalition of partners and the building of strong alliances to improve learning and graduation rates. The writers also make a strong case for the importance of parent and community engagement, which the literature has demonstrated have an important impact on student achievement.

Glaze, Mattingley, and Andrews all played pivotal roles in the implementation of Ontario's school and district improvement strategies. It was my privilege to work with them as colleagues in those efforts. As dedicated and skilled individuals who worked extensively with educators and schools, they know the importance of practitioner perspective on what really works in bringing about continuing improvement in teaching and learning. They discuss the need for a strong focus on literacy, numeracy, and other foundation skills and a strong orientation to excellence with equity. The use of data for decision making, developing strong leadership, assuming accountability for student learning, and using effective instructional practices are all essential components. As well, the need to engage the larger community in improving learning is fully explored. Other key strategies to build character and develop citizenship skills are discussed as integral to the outcomes needed for society. Equally important is the fact that they are asking you, their colleagues, to engage in the extension and refinement of knowledge on practices that improve student outcomes, broadly conceived.

One of the many practical strengths of this book is the wide array of specific interventions strategies and proven practices that can be used at all stages and transition points in schools. There is no shortage of successful practices at our disposal, but these interventions must be focused and intentional. This book highlights many of the carefully designed supports for students who are not succeeding, with the strong message that failure can no longer be tolerated. It is a book by practitioners for practitioners.

This book distils many, many years of experience and a great deal of wisdom in terms that all educators can understand and use. It's my pleasure to be able to endorse and support this work. I know all readers will find it valuable.

Dr. Ben Levin
Professor, The Ontario Institute for Studies in Education

Preface

Educators today are strategically placed to realize both excellence and equity in outcomes for students—to raise the bar for all students and to close the achievement gaps. Variations in learning should no longer be attributed to background factors. Indeed, schools must remove barriers, empower students, and create the conditions necessary to ensure success for all.

This call to action is not an abstract theory of what could be, but rather an approach that educators are already taking in their districts, schools, and classrooms—an approach that is already producing significant results. Educators are already convinced that they cannot give up now or show signs of disenchantment or discouragement. They are aware of their role in building a civil society, focusing on results, and advocating for students from diverse groups and those who live in poverty. In other words, educators are fully aware that the focus of education in the next few years has to be on removing the barriers that prevent an improvement in graduation rates. This mission is very important to the students from groups that have a history of failure or of dropping out of school. The need to build alliances and coalitions to support learning and to ensure that schools serve the needs of all students will take center stage. Politicians and parents alike will continue to demand that schools use the strategies at their disposal to raise the bar for all students and close achievement gaps for those who have not been successful in the past.

The litmus test or, indeed, the question we must ask ourselves is this: Can we afford to replicate the status quo? Under our watch, can there be "throwaway" kids? Will our society remain competitive in the global arena if a significant number of students cannot read, write, or do mathematics? Can we accept the fact that a large number of students will not graduate from high school? Can we, as educators, tolerate the waste of human potential if some students leave our schools without the education they deserve?

There is a cacophony of voices demanding improvement in the number of students who graduate from schools. There are persuasive arguments for a focus on the moral, economic, social justice, and human rights imperatives of schooling. Educators are taking this clarion call very seriously in their efforts to live up to the promise of making education a driving force for societal improvement and global competitiveness. Improving graduation rates will depend on educators and policy makers evaluating the effectiveness of the strategies that they are currently using from kindergarten to Grade 12, and revisiting the criteria for assessing the effectiveness of learning environments. It will require deep commitment to action and to monitoring what effect the implementation of their strategies is having for the success of our students. Student success, in terms of graduation, is not only dependent on the quality of instruction and educational experiences in high schools; it is also dependent on the strong foundation of knowledge, skills, and attitudes that is laid. It is also dependent on the establishment of high expectations for the success of all students beginning in the early years of a child's education.

The most important role of schools today is to ensure academic engagement and achievement from kindergarten to Grade 12. Our schools are uniquely positioned to equip our young people with the skills they require to be successful, contributing adults in our society. This challenge, however, is constant throughout the full breadth of the child's educational journey; specific interventions must be in place at all stages and transition points along the continuum. It is critical that educators recognize that improved graduation rates are dependent on improving teaching and learning throughout students' journey from kindergarten to the end of high school. Waiting until high school to challenge and engage students or to implement intervention strategies is too late. Success is dependent on a whole-system approach at the district, school, and classroom levels, across the grades, beginning with strategies that are implemented at the first indication that students are not performing according to the established standards and criteria. These strategies must be focused and intentional with specific, appropriate, and targeted supports for students who are not succeeding. A strong safety net must be in place to give students more chances to achieve graduation. In the study *Unlocking Potential for Learning* (Campbell, Fullan, & Glaze, 2006), it was clearly shown that sustained improvement in student achievement depends on schools, districts, and provinces adopting an aligned approach that builds the capacity of teachers, school leaders, boards, district leaders, parents, and community allies. *High School Graduation: K–12 Strategies That Work* provides a comprehensive approach to school and district improvement using proven strategies to enhance student achievement and increase graduation rates.

There are many evidence-based approaches that are being implemented in many jurisdictions across the world. Those promising practices must be adopted, and strategies that do not work must be abandoned. Many jurisdictions are proving that all students can learn and succeed given time and proper supports. This means that it is necessary to ensure that all teachers and principals have access to these approaches and should be encouraged to improve on their knowledge base in an effort to sustain the gains that have already been made. Our experience is that it takes different approaches and renewed effort to bring about improvement at different stages along the journey, especially as one gets closer to the target. What we also know is that this work has to be done with a sense of urgency. The fact is that the students cannot wait—nor will their societies, as each country strives to take its place in the global economy.

In Ontario, improving graduation rates has been a key priority. Over the past nine years, continuous progress has been achieved. The research-informed strategies outlined in this book are based on the firsthand experiences of the authors who were provincial leaders in the development and implementation of Ontario's improvement strategy for kindergarten through Grade 12. This book provides an improvement framework for school district leaders, school administrators, classroom teachers, and policy makers. It documents the instructional strategies and improvement processes used to bring about the changes that have resulted in continuous improvement in student outcomes.

Education benefits all members of the community, and making gains in achievement requires the support of all those who have a vested interest in this critical undertaking. The importance of developing community alliances and building coalitions to support learning is important; schools cannot do this alone. Through the development of networks, the sharing of promising practices, and the support of one another, schools and their communities keep the momentum for improvement alive.

High School Graduation is a detailed, comprehensive resource for the principals, teachers, superintendents, directors, and policy makers whose primary quest is to improve their schools and districts and to help all students achieve at higher levels and graduate from high school. This book outlines high-impact, research-informed strategies that have been demonstrated to improve student achievement. The authors have provided practical processes, tools, and templates that will assist jurisdictions to achieve their improvement goals. Sample tools such as templates for improvement planning are included.

There is, indeed, a sense of urgency in improving student achievement. Schleicher (2006) asserts that, regardless of where we live in the world or where we stand in terms of development, the ability to compete in the fast-growing economy with demands for high-level skills hinges on significant improvements in the quality of schooling outcomes and a more equitable distribution of learning opportunities.

In 2011, the Organisation for Economic Co-operation and Development (OECD) said that Canadian students do well not only on the Programme for International Student Assessment (PISA); they do so despite their socioeconomic status, first language, or status as Aboriginal Canadians or recent immigrants. OECD stated that Canada has achieved success within a system that accommodates a diverse student population. Researchers examined Canada's success through an in-depth look at the province of Ontario and validated our strategy, which they described as combining a demand for excellence with extensive capacity building, and fostering a climate of trust and mutual respect among all stakeholders (OECD, 2011).

Teachers, principals, and all those who work in schools are to be commended for the progress they have already made. But as time progresses, we cannot rest on our laurels. We know we can do better. We know that we can raise our expectations of the number of students who can graduate from high school successfully with our guidance, support, and effective teaching.

As countries across the globe focus on educational improvement, there is an expressed need by educators to discover and implement the strategies that improve student learning and achievement. This book documents Ontario's success story and provides a reflection on the reasons the approaches that were selected, from a field of possibilities, worked. Educators across the world will find that many of the processes described can work in their own contexts. It also helps that the Ontario system has received external recognition and validation for its focus on excellence and equity and for closing achievement gaps.

We invite educators to share our enthusiasm for the future of education. We certainly have the will and the skills to improve graduation rates. This requires inspired, persistent performance and motivation, and an enduring belief that our efforts do, indeed, enhance life chances. Our confidence is based on recognition of what we have already achieved. We know we can do even better. We must keep the momentum alive. Improving graduation rates is a mission that is possible and one that we embrace with confidence.

References

Campbell, C., Fullan, M., and Glaze, A. (2006). *Unlocking potential for learning: Effective district-wide strategies to raise student achievement in literacy and numeracy.* Toronto: Ontario Ministry of Education.

Ontario Ministry of Education. (2011). *Ontario schools: Kindergarten to Grade 12: Policy and program requirements.* Toronto: Author.

Organisation for Economic Co-operation and Development (OECD). (2010, December 6). *Education: What students know and what can they do?* [Video file]. Retrieved from http://www.youtube.com/watch?feature=player_embedded&v=0D-JpL5fFgc

Organisation for Economic Co-operation and Development (OECD). (2011), *Education at a glance 2011: OECD indicators.* Paris: Author. http://www.oecd-ilibrary.org/education/education-at-a-glance-2011_eag-2011-en

Schleicher, A. (2006). *The economics of knowledge: Why education is key for Europe's success* (The Lisbon Council Policy Brief). Brussels: The Lisbon Council.

Acknowledgments

We extend heartfelt gratitude to Ontario educators with whom we have worked over the years to improve student outcomes. The strategies we describe in this book and the lessons we have all learned together have contributed to the gains that Ontario has made on the world stage. Ontario teachers, principals, policy makers, parent and community members deserve many encomiums for the progress that has been demonstrated over the years. Ours was truly a team effort—one in which we contributed to each other's professional learning and motivation to constantly raise the bar of performance.

We cannot thank all of the individuals who have played key roles in the improvement agenda. We are compelled, however, to thank Michael Fullan, Ben Levin, George Zegarac, Mary Jean Gallagher and all the staff of the Literacy and Numeracy Secretariat Ministry of Education, and the school boards across Ontario. We also recognize the contribution of Nathalie Carrier, Hilary Edelstein, Sabina Persaud, Robyn Reid, and Jacqueline Sohn.

Specifically,

Avis wishes to thank her husband, Peter Bailey, for his keen insights, helpful critiques and tireless support of her work and career.

Ruth thanks her husband John and son Billy for their constant support and encouragement. In addition Ruth would like to personally thank Avis Glaze for her vision and passion to improve educational outcomes for all students and for inviting her to work by her side at the Literacy and Numeracy Secretariat.

Rob thanks his family and friends for their ongoing support. On a professional level, there are seven very important leaders who have made a tremendous difference for him and for the countless students whose lives they have enhanced. He would like to thank Barry O'Connor, Grant Clarke, and Kit Rankin for their inspirational leadership in the early years of the Student Success strategy. He also thanks Avis Glaze, Sylvia Terpstra, Mary Jean Gallagher, and Kevin Costante for the work they have done to ensure that the students always came first and that the supports they needed were optimized to the fullest extent possible.

We thank the following expert reviewers of the manuscript for their excellent feedback and recommendations:

Susan Kessler
Executive Principal Hunters Lane High School
Nashville, TN

John P. Rice
Director of Math, Science and Technology Education
North Syracuse Central School District

Dr. Richard Rutledge
Assistant Principal
Arab High School

Kelly VanLaeken
Principal, Ruben A. Cirillo High School
Gananda Central School District

Finally, we thank Professor Ben Levin of the Ontario Institute for Studies in Education, University of Toronto, for writing the forward to this book.

About the Authors

 **Dr. Avis Glaze** is a well-known international leader in education. As Ontario's first chief student achievement officer and founding CEO of the Literacy and Numeracy Secretariat, she played a pivotal role in improving student achievement in Ontario. Avis is currently the founder and president of her company, Eduquest International, Inc.

Avis has worked at all levels of the education system—from classroom teacher to superintendent of schools, director of education, and education officer. She was research coordinator with the Ontario Women's Directorate of the Ministry of Labour. She also served as Ontario's education commissioner and senior adviser to the Minister of Education.

Avis was commissioner on the Ontario Royal Commission on Learning, influencing the direction of education in the province. She represented the Canadian government with education reform in South Africa and at the UNESCO conference on inclusive education in Riga, Latvia. As well, she has worked with educators in Australia, New Zealand, England, Finland, Norway, the Netherlands, Ireland, Scotland, Germany, Singapore, the Caribbean, and many parts of the United States.

Avis has received honorary doctorates from several Canadian universities, including her alma mater, the University of Toronto. She has won more than 40 awards for outstanding contribution to education, including Educator of the Year, the Sandford D. McDonnell Lifetime Achievement Award for Character Education offered by the Character Education Partnership in the United States, and the Order of Ontario.

She has been involved in a landmark research on Ontario high school girls and has written many articles on topics as diverse as leadership, career development, character education, diversity, equity, and inclusive education. She co-authored *Towards Freedom: The African-Canadian Experience* (with Ken Alexander) and *Breaking Barriers; Excellence and Equity for All* (Glaze, Mattingley, & Levin, 2012).

 **Ruth Mattingley** has provided leadership in education provincially, nationally, and internationally. Ruth was formerly the senior executive officer at the Literacy and Numeracy Secretariat, Ontario Ministry of Education. In this role, Ruth worked closely with Ontario's chief student achievement officer, Dr. Avis Glaze, to develop Ontario's provincial strategy for improving achievement in literacy and numeracy for elementary school students. Ruth also worked closely with school districts and schools across Ontario as they developed strategic plans that focused on improving student achievement. Ruth is currently an associate with Edu-quest International.

Prior to joining the Literacy and Numeracy Secretariat, Ruth was a superintendent of education with the Lambton Kent District School Board with portfolios ranging from curriculum development and implementation, special education, and human resources, as well as supervising a family of schools. Ruth also has experience as an elementary school principal, classroom, and special education teacher.

Ruth has worked with educational leaders both within Canada and internationally with a focus on district and school improvement planning, high-impact strategies for improving student achievement, equity and diversity, and improving student achievement in schools in challenging circumstances. Ruth has written numerous articles and recently co-authored *Breaking Barriers: Excellence and Equity for All* (Glaze, Mattingley, & Levin, 2012).

Ruth is a past president of the Ontario Public Supervisory Officers Association (OPSOA) and a past president of the Canadian Association of School Administrators (CASA). She was the recipient of the OPSOA Distinguished Leadership Award and the Ontario recipient of the CASA Excel Leadership Award.

 **Rob Andrews** is the director of the Student Success/Learning to 18 Strategic Implementation, Innovation and Support branch of the Student Achievement Division at the Ontario Ministry of Education. He has also served as a teacher, vice principal, principal, and superintendent of education with the Kawartha Pine Ridge District School Board (Peterborough, Ontario) with responsibility for student success, alternative education, and secondary school reform. Rob spent an additional year serving as an education officer for the Strategic Policy Branch of the Student Success Branch at the Ontario Ministry of Education in 2005–2006. He has been involved with Ontario's Student Success initiative since its inception in 2003 and has worked in this capacity with directors of education, supervisory officers, Student Success leaders, secondary school principals, Ministry of Education staff, teacher teams, and consultants to develop and implement professional supports. With an emphasis on the four "pillars" of student success, these supports focus on the leadership, facilitation and strategies that allow for broad changes in secondary school programs, transitions to secondary schools, supporting students at risk, and changing school and system culture with respect to serving all students. He has also been engaged in planning for the enhanced use of instructional technology in the teaching and learning process.

Rob has been involved in school and community collaboration and has engaged key stakeholders in the analysis of system data, in the performance of baseline establishment, gap analysis, goal and target setting, strategic planning, implementation, and monitoring for initiatives related to the Student Success portfolio. He has been a secondary school teacher and administrator since 1987 and has extensive experience with adult and alternative education. He holds a master of education degree in educational administration and has been a supervisory officer in Ontario since 2006.

1

Results Without Rancor or Ranking

The Ontario Improvement Strategy

Countries across the world are focused on improving educational outcomes for their students. Yet despite these efforts, many students are still leaving school without a high school diploma. This seriously disadvantages our youth and, quite frankly, puts the future of our communities and countries in jeopardy. In the current knowledge-based economy, our greatest resource is our children. As educators, we owe it to students, parents, communities, and future generations to establish effective pathways to graduation.

Our quest for educational excellence with equity must be relentless. Building and developing a robust publicly funded education system is a challenge we must all embrace. This is our best guarantee for realizing the future we owe to the students in our schools today. Working toward the goal of providing every child with a graduation diploma is a vision that must become reality.

It has long been recognized that a high-quality education system has a profound impact on the well-being and prosperity of a country. As early as in 2003, Levin outlined the cost to a nation when the education system is inadequate. He states that countries will experience

- foregone national income,
- foregone tax revenues for the support of government services,
- increased demand on social services,
- increased crime, and
- poorer levels of health.

From a moral perspective, we must employ strategies that help every student to graduate, but as Levin points out, there are other compelling reasons to improve graduation rates.

Research has clearly shown that early school achievement, especially in reading and writing, is one of the greatest predictors of future success. We need to ensure that we provide our students with the skills necessary to succeed in a knowledge economy. Student success is dependent on a sound foundation in literacy. In one jurisdiction, researchers learned that the local penitentiary predicts, with accuracy, the number of prison cells that will be required by the number of students in the public schools who are reading below grade level in the second grade (Hale, 2004). It is critical that educators recognize that improved graduation rates are dependent on improving teaching and learning throughout our students' journey from kindergarten to graduation. The responsibility to ensure that more students graduate from high school does not begin at the secondary level. It begins when students enter elementary school, where the focus has to be on having students read at grade level. There is ample evidence that well over 90% of children can read by the end of Grade 1 with intentionality, good teaching, and proper supports.

In Ontario, students in Grades 3, 6, and 9 are required to participate in annual provincial assessments. The assessments are administered by the Education Quality and Accountability Office (EQAO), an organization that was established to be arm's length from the government and accountable to the public, to assess and report on the quality of education in the province. EQAO has gathered information regarding the achievement of students as measured by the provincial assessments since 1996–1997. In tracking student progress over the past 14 years, it has been shown that students who do well on the provincial assessment in the primary (Grades 1–3) and junior (Grades 4–6) divisions will most likely maintain their high level of achievement in secondary school. EQAO (2011) has found that 92% of students that met the provincial standard in both Grades 3 and 6 again met the standard in the

Grade 9 academic mathematics course, and 77% met it again in the Grade 9 applied mathematics course. It is evident from the research conducted that ensuring that students are successful in the early years of their schooling will give them a greater chance of obtaining a high school diploma.

The greatest resource a country has is its youth. The future well-being, prosperity, and global competitiveness of a country are dependent on high-quality education for its children. If students are to survive and thrive in the 21st century, it is essential for educational systems to implement the high-impact strategies that contribute to student success in school and equip them to be contributing members of society. Educators have a moral imperative to help all students achieve at higher levels and to help them prepare for the wide spectrum of postsecondary destinations that are available to them. This reality has resulted in school systems around the world making improved student learning and dropout prevention key priorities. Improving graduation rates is a goal to which all publicly funded education systems should aspire.

It is essential for all districts to look at their K–12 continuum to ensure that students are not falling through the cracks. One cannot talk about improving graduation rates without first examining the quality of the educational system, from kindergarten right through to Grade 12. As Curran, Balfanz, and Herzog (2007) point out, "A high percentage of dropouts send distress signals in the middle grades, long before they actually drop out of school" (p. 28). It is critical that educators recognize that improved graduation rates are dependent on improving teaching and learning in all grades. Too often, we blame secondary schools for the dropout rate instead of recognizing that the foundation in the early years is critical to future success. Waiting until high school to challenge and engage students or to implement intervention strategies is too late. "For many students, lagging achievement evidenced as early as fourth grade appears to be a powerful predictor of rates of high school and college graduation, as well as lifetime earnings" (McKinsey & Company, 2009, p. 5).

There is a worldwide trend and a multitude of voices demanding accountability in education. Many countries are currently engaged in education reform and system improvement. Political leaders around the world have made improved student learning and dropout prevention a priority. To achieve the goal of lowering dropout rates and improving achievement results for all students, educators will need support and resources that will provide them with proven processes and strategies.

It is within this context that we share the Ontario experience in improving student achievement in elementary schools and high school graduation rates without the ranking of schools or the rancour that often accompanies educational reform. Ontario is considered across the world as one of the fastest-improving systems. What is most noteworthy is that this has been achieved in the context of Ontario's diversity. Ontario is one of the largest and most diverse provinces in Canada, attracting the majority of immigrants that come to this country each year from more than 200 countries.

The Canadian Context

Canada is one of the few countries in the industrialized world without a national department of education; there are, rather, 13 different education systems for each of our 10 provinces and three territories. Some aspects of education governance are, however, determined centrally. For example, the Indian Act gives the federal government responsibility for Aboriginal education on reserves, while the Constitution protects the rights of minoritized groups. Catholics are considered a minority under the Constitution with the right to operate their own publicly funded education system. The Constitution also protects the right of minorities of the two official languages, English and French, to operate English- and French-language district school boards.

The Extent of Ontario's Diversity

In Ontario, children from immigrant backgrounds, low-income homes, and those with special education needs or with other challenges are improving their achievement consistently. This proves that the strategies are working. Low-performing schools have been reduced to an all-time low and "static" schools, where results had flatlined, are doing better than they have ever done. Excellence and equity have become hallmarks of this school system.

When examining Ontario's results in PISA in 2009, it was evident not only that Ontario is one of the highest performing jurisdictions, but, while achieving excellence, the province is also reducing gaps in achievement. PISA confirmed this improvement, stating that Ontario is among the few jurisdictions in the world that demonstrate both higher achievement in reading and a smaller performance gap between high- and low-income students when compared to the OECD average (EQAO, 2010).

Ontario has been able to achieve continuous improvement in closing achievement gaps when working with students from a wide range of backgrounds. Ontario is the home of 40% of Canada's 34 million people. It is Canada's most diverse province and continues to be the province of choice for newcomers to Canada: 60% of the 225,000 immigrants who come to Canada annually settle in Ontario. This province has 2.1 million students in four provincially operated education governance systems: English public, English Catholic, French public, and French Catholic. Data from the Ministry of Education website (www.edu.gov.on.ca), show that approximately 1.4 million students attend Ontario's 4,000 elementary schools, and approximately 700,000 attend more than 850 secondary schools. The 2006 Statistics Canada census indicates that 28.3% of Ontario's population are immigrants, with 4.8% arriving in the last five years. As well, 22.8% of Ontario's population are visible minorities. When compared to U.S. jurisdictions, it has the population equivalent to Illinois, Pennsylvania, or Ohio, the fifth, sixth, and seventh most populous states.

Between 2001 and 2006, Ontario's Aboriginal population grew nearly five times faster than the non-Aboriginal population. Ontarians reported more than 200 languages as their mother tongue. By 2017, about one fifth of our population will be members of diverse faith communities, including Islam, Hinduism, Buddhism, and Judaism, in addition to a growing number of individuals without a religious affiliation (Ontario Ministry of Education, 2009).

Ontario is also diverse geographically. There are more than 1 million square kilometers of land with large urban centers (e.g., Greater Toronto Area) and remote rural and northern areas. Ontario has not only improved achievement as measured by provincial assessments and graduation rates, but has also been among the top performers in international assessments. The Ontario strategies that have worked in such a diverse context are applicable and replicable in other jurisdictions. Ensuring international comparability was a key reform strategy in Ontario. We have long recognized the importance of looking beyond our borders to learn with and from others. We have benefited from the experiences, successes, and failures of other jurisdictions. As well, we have used international research extensively to broaden our approach and deepen our understanding of how children learn and what it takes to help all children become successful.

Three key beliefs drove educational reform in Ontario:

- It takes clear vision and persistent resolve to transform the educational system.
- Public education is the foundation of democracy.
- Excellence and equity go hand in hand.

A Clear Vision and Persistent Resolve

In Ontario, there has been clarity of direction, persistent resolve, and an enduring sense of mission to transform the educational system. The government of the day placed education at the center of its mandate with a firm commitment to improvement. The underlying foundation for reform rested with a commitment to build capacity among educators at all levels to improve teaching and learning. The vision for the Ontario educational system was one of excellence with equity, ensuring that all students, regardless of gender, race, socioeconomic status, or other human rights factors achieve at higher levels. The strategy focused on three key strategic goals adopted by the Ministry of Education for all schools:

- Increased student achievement
- Reduced gaps in performance
- Increased public confidence in public education

These goals were the catalyst for the reform of K–12 education in Ontario. A critical aspect of the Ontario strategy was that change efforts would respect of the professional knowledge of educators. Alliances were developed between the Ministry of Education, district school boards, and professional organizations (e.g., teachers unions, principal and superintendent organizations, and parent, student, and trustee associations). The Ontario strategy built good will, affirmed the professionalism of teachers, and enhanced the motivation of all who work in education to improve our schools.

A sense of urgency was ignited within all those charged with improving the school system with the notion that the students cannot wait. It was recognized that educating all children to the highest level possible was our moral imperative. This resolve to improve the outcomes for all

The strategies outlined in this book resulted in continuous improvement in Ontario's Graduation rates:

Year	Graduation Rates
2003–2004	68%
2004–2005	71%
2005–2006	73%
2006–2007	75%
2007–2008	77%
2008–2009	79%
2009–2010	81%
2010–2011	82%

Source: www.edu.gov.on.ca

students was sustained through positive pressure and intensive support. Ambitious targets for student achievement were established while, at the same time, educators received a variety of supports to strengthen their professional practice. Administrators and teachers were provided with ongoing professional learning opportunities, resources were developed to support classroom instruction, class sizes were reduced to provide more individualized instruction, and ministry staff supported improvement efforts at the school level. The Ontario strategy recognized that to improve our schools, we must invest in people, support them, and develop their professional expertise.

Excellence and Equity Go Hand in Hand

We recognize that educators can enhance the life chances of our diverse population and prepare our young people to participate fully in Canadian society as well as in the global economy. In Ontario, with our belief that factors such as poverty should not truncate the life chances of students, we have used focused intervention strategies to ensure that all children learn regardless of personal and socio-economic factors. As a province, we have demonstrated that results can be achieved without alienating our teachers and principals or without imposing punitive approaches and negative sanctions. In fact, our strategy engaged educators fully and reaffirmed their sense of education as a moral imperative.

Turning the Ontario System Around

In the early years of 2000, the times in Ontario were described as turbulent at best. Labor unrest and tension-filled relationships between government and educators led to eroding confidence in the public system and low morale among teachers. Many educators felt that there was a climate of fear and resentment, with teachers experiencing a range of emotions from anger to despair. The teaching profession itself seemed to be suffering from a damaged self-concept. Many chose to retire as soon as they possibly could. Fewer individuals wanted to enter the teaching profession or to assume leadership positions. The system had become focused on operations and fiscal management rather than on instructional leadership and student achievement. Not surprisingly, student achievement had flatlined, and enrollment in private schools was on the rise. From all accounts, the system was in a state of crisis.

Then the new Liberal government took office and made a strong commitment to improving the Ontario education system. The first step in realizing excellence would require that every student in Ontario develop reading, writing, mathematical, and comprehension skills at a higher level by the age of 12. Progress would be measured by ensuring that 75% of students reached the provincial standard of a "B," or 70%, within a specified time frame. At the secondary level, a provincial target was also set—namely, that 85% of students would graduate from high school by 2010–2011.

To ensure system reform, the government consulted with leading researchers, policy makers. and practitioners to develop a strategy with tight timelines and with the following key components:

1. A small number of ambitious goals

2. A "guiding coalition," including the premier and the minister of education, to monitor and support change

3. A respected educator with experience at all levels of the system appointed as chief student achievement officer to "champion" the initiative

4. High standards and expectations, with a focus on both excellence and equity

5. Investment in capacity building at all levels, with an emphasis on instructional effectiveness

6. Investment in leadership development

7. The use of research-informed, high-impact strategies to improve achievement

8. The use of data and authentic assessment to improve practice

9. The implementation of nonpunitive intervention strategies to improve low performing schools

10. Paying attention to the distracters, such as collective agreements and unnecessary bureaucracy, to protect the focus on the core priorities

The approach taken for this massive reform effort involved engagement and alignment at all levels, which included the provincial (state), district, school, and classroom levels.

At the provincial level, policies were established and resources allocated to provide much needed support to schools and districts. Provincial leaders sought input from school board administrators, teachers' unions, trustees, student and parent groups, and other stakeholders as they shaped the provincial strategy. District school boards were expected to establish local improvement teams and to develop, implement, and monitor improvement plans. The province provided student achievement officers (SAOs) to support improvement at the elementary school level and funds for student success leaders (SSLs) to facilitate change in high schools. Finally, at the school level, supports were provided to ensure capacity building that would strengthen instructional practice. Small amounts of funds were provided to purchase necessary resources and free teachers up so they could share their expertise and plan collaboratively for improved student learning. This comprehensive provincial reform strategy is explained in greater detail in subsequent chapters.

The result of this effort can be seen in improved provincial achievement scores and higher graduation rates. Other obvious signs of progress included

- a clear focus on improving student achievement,
- improved morale and confidence in the government's improvement agenda,
- a pervasive focus on capacity building and job-embedded professional learning,
- consistent improvement among schools in socioeconomically challenging circumstances,
- previously underachieving groups increasing their performance significantly, and
- a surge in confidence among educators in their ability to improve their schools.

The strategies used to achieve these results are well documented in current research and have proven to be effective in improving achievement for students throughout the province.

As a result of the reform strategy, Ontario has also seen a cultural shift where educators are more actively involved in the improvement process, resulting in improved morale and stronger professional learning communities. Table 1.1 is a comparison of the provincial climate before the reform strategy was implemented to the current climate.

Table 1.1   The Change in Provincial Climate

Before	Now
• Disparate goals and priorities	• Clear and strategic goals aligned • Specific student achievement targets
• Multiple disjointed initiatives	• Selected high-impact strategies
• Isolated, ad hoc professional development	• Team focused and job-embedded professional learning
• Limited reliance on research and data	• Research based and data driven
• Focus on compliance	• Focus on horizontal accountability
• Poor morale and lack of involvement	• High motivation and commitment to sustain gains and achieve continuous improvement
• Flatlined achievement levels	• Continuous improvement in student achievement and graduation rates
• Inequity in achievement results	• The narrowing of achievement gaps
• Focus on basic skills	• Emphasis on 21st century, higher order critical and thinking skills, and character development

Starting With Literacy

In recognizing the importance of literacy as a foundation for learning, success in school, and future career choices, the Ontario government created the Literacy and Numeracy Secretariat (the Secretariat) with a mandate to drive change and create a new way of working with the school districts to bring about improvement in the schools. It was the responsibility of the Secretariat to provide strategic leadership in building strong linkages and alliances with system partners to support learning. Dr. Avis Glaze, a veteran educator, was chosen to be Ontario's first chief student achievement officer and CEO of the Secretariat with Ruth Mattingley as the senior executive officer. Rob Andrews, our third author, later became the director of the Student Success/Learning to 18 Strategic Implementation, Innovation and Support in the Student Achievement Division of the Ontario Ministry of Education.

The Secretariat moved quickly to forge consensus around the philosophy, modus operandi, resources, strategies, and tools that would be needed to ensure success for all students.

The primary goal of the Secretariat was to work collaboratively with the school districts to

- create a renewed focus on literacy and numeracy,
- share promising practices among schools and districts,

- extend the knowledge base of the profession,
- increase capacity to support learning, and
- engage parents, school councils, business, community members, and trustees to further support the student achievement goals.

Early on, the Secretariat recognized that a "one-size-fits-all" approach would not work. A range of strategies were implemented to address the diverse needs of district school boards and schools across the province. For change to happen and be sustained, it is critical to have ownership at all levels. Relying solely on top-down approaches has not proved to be effective in the long term. The Secretariat's approach was to work alongside districts and schools, providing a range of supports and capacity building for them to take ownership for their own improvement efforts.

The work of the Secretariat was soon being lauded across the world. The Canadian Language and Literacy Network (CLLRNet), an independent consultancy asked by the government to evaluate the Secretariat's effectiveness, said that the Secretariat's efforts, in partnership with school boards, had resulted in a significant shift in the culture of Ontario schools that is focused on enabling the success of all students. The evaluation concluded that the model used by the Secretariat was effective and should continue. They stated that "over its brief history, Ontario's Literacy and Numeracy Secretariat has had a major, and primarily highly positive, impact on Ontario's education system" (CLLRNet, 2009, p. 11).

The Secretariat successfully engaged teachers, principals, and supervisory officers in sharing ownership and responsibility for the achievement of the goals. As well, the Secretariat successfully entrenched the notion that "business as usual" would not bring about the results needed to improve student learning and close gaps in achievement.

A strong commitment to research, evidence-based inquiry, and data-informed decision making was critical to the success of the strategy. The Secretariat launched an innovative series of monographs, titled "What Works: Research Into Practice," as well as highly popular webcasts and web conferences. Using research-informed, high-impact instructional strategies has resulted in improved student achievement at all levels.

Improving Graduation Rates

Ontario, much like other jurisdictions, was deeply concerned about the number of students leaving high school prior to graduation. Roughly 25% of Ontario's students were not graduating from high school (King, 2004). In Ontario, we looked for innovative ways to evolve traditional practices to improve support for students while they are at school and to create the conditions for their successful graduation and transition to postsecondary destinations.

Determined to improve the graduation rates in Ontario, the government established an ambitious target. They set a goal that specified that 85% of those who had entered Grade 9 in a given year (cohort group) would graduate. To accomplish this goal, the Ministry established the Student Success/Learning to 18 strategy and supported it with resources, including policy, legislation, and human, media, and monetary resources. The Ministry created internal divisions to support the strategy and the various compo-nents and pillars. Assistance was also needed in the schools. Every school board and authority received funding for a dedicated SSL and was provided with an annual budget with which to support the initiatives related to each pillar. In 2005, the Ministry also introduced the SST, a secondary school teaching role that was funded above the grants that school boards normally received based on the number of students enrolled. These teachers were expected to serve as advocates for students deemed to be "at risk," to track, counsel, and work on behalf of these students to optimize their chances of success.

Three themes shape the secondary (high school) reform effort in Ontario:

1. The importance of building foundational skills in literacy and numeracy

2. The need to provide a more explicit and richer menu of programs

3. The need to attending to the individual well-being of students as a precursor to achievement

The Ontario Student Success/Learning to 18 Strategy introduced four "pillars" of student success based on these themes:

- **Literacy**: The primary intent of the literacy strategy was to ensure that students graduate with the essential literacy skills for life. The literacy strategy consisted of professional development and training and the development of literacy support materials. The Ontario Literacy Course was also introduced as a support for students who had been unsuccessful in passing the provincial literacy test, which is a prerequisite for graduation.

- **Numeracy**: The focus in this pillar was to ensure that students develop the mathematics skills and understanding they need to reach their full potential in the 21st century. A variety of projects were introduced to help improve mathematics instruction in secondary schools. The numeracy strategy focused on teacher training, structured lesson design, and resource development for a variety of learning styles.

- **Program Pathways**: This part of the strategy focused on the creation of program options that reflect quality choices for students bound for different postsecondary destinations. The specific strategies include grouping course selections, designing the specialization of course content to reflect areas of focus, increases in experiential learning opportunities that connect curriculum to relevant experiences outside of the school environment, certification, and the recording and tracking of these to further support students. The creation of the Specialist High Skills Major (SHSM) included a special designation on a students' graduation diploma, as well as the furthering of strong partnerships with employers, apprenticeship organizations, and colleges.

- **Community Culture and Caring**: This pillar evolved to address the variety of nonacademic or program challenges that create barriers for many students as they move through the education system. The strategy has focused on the engagement of students in their school communities and addresses students in transition as well as targeted groups that demonstrate low engagement.

With each of the pillars in place, Ontario's secondary schools have been undergoing a remarkable transformation. An investigation in Chapter 5 of the development of the initiative and of each pillar serves to illustrate how the Ontario government has been able to work collaboratively with school districts across Ontario to improve student success rates so that 93,000 more students have graduated from high school over the past eight years. These dramatic improvements are being recognized across the world. They are significant because many people see the improvement of secondary schools as a near intractable proposition. Because of the Student Success strategy, the life chances of students are being enhanced.

Where Are We Now?

There is a sense of urgency in the province that is founded on our belief that children cannot wait for slow-moving improvement. Educators have recommitted themselves to their moral responsibility to ensure that all children succeed. They are working together to ensure school improvement and are setting ambitious achievement targets for their students. Schools are implementing research-informed, high-impact strategies to meet the unique needs of their students. Educators are tracking progress and revising their practice when necessary.

Through a combination of positive pressure and support, achievement results have improved. More students are graduating from high school than ever before. Ontario is achieving results that are comparable to or surpassing many high-achieving countries across the globe.

And by Ontario's own standards, progress has been sustained, the results are transparent and, the gains are validated by external bodies such as the OECD.

In sum, the following represents the essence of the Ontario strategy:

- Ensuring dialogue and engagement with all stakeholders

  - ✓ Forging consensus
  - ✓ Developing a common sense of purpose
  - ✓ Building commitment and motivation

- Providing positive pressure and support
- Supporting and guiding school improvement planning
- Implementing high-impact strategies
- Requiring deep implementation and monitoring of progress
- Providing targeted resources
- Facilitating capacity building at all levels of the system
- Promoting teacher collaboration
- Conducting assessments of district and school effectiveness
- Focusing on professional accountability
- Insisting on excellence and equity
- Supporting community outreach and engagement
- Ensuring international comparability

The challenges that Ontario faced when seeking to improve student achievement and graduation rates are not unique. Across the globe, there has been a growing demand for accountability in education and improved results. Meeting the needs of a diverse population is prevalent not only in Ontario, but in most jurisdictions as well. We have similar concerns, such as improving outcomes for students living in poverty and minoritized groups that have historically underperformed. By examining current research, policies, and practices from around the world, Ontario developed a comprehensive reform strategy that continues to meet the needs of a diverse population.

The authors of this book have all been instrumental in implementing the government's agenda while serving in the Ministry of Education in different capacities. One of us had the distinct honor of being appointed by the government as Ontario's first chief student achievement officer and CEO of the Literacy and Numeracy Secretariat. The mandate was to establish the Secretariat to drive change and achieve results with a sense of urgency. Another of us played an important role in the Secretariat as associate to this role, and the third served as director in the Ministry of Education, continuing the development and implementation of the strategy for the reform of secondary schools.

We take pride in the fact that Ontario has been able to achieve excellent results without punitive measures or the ranking of schools. We have created conditions to ensure that educational leaders and teachers develop the capacity and the motivation required to deliver on the education agenda. In Ontario, teachers and principals now feel that they have the skill, the will, and the necessary determination to take a system to the zenith of its possibilities.

We are confident that educators around the globe will discover a range of strategies in this book that are applicable to their circumstances. Ontario's success was based on the premise that one size does not fit all. It is therefore important that policy makers and educators critically examine the strategies in light of their district's needs and context.

References

Campbell, C., Fullan, M., & Glaze, A. (2006). *Unlocking potential for learning: Effective district-wide strategies to raise student achievement in literacy and numeracy.* Toronto: Ontario Ministry of Education. Retrieved from http://www.edu.gov.on.ca/eng/literacynumeracy/inspire/research/projectreport_full.pdf

Canadian Language and Literacy Research Network (CLLRNet). (2009, Spring). *The impact of the Literacy and Numeracy Secretariat: Changes in Ontario's education system.* (Report for the Ontario Ministry of Education). Toronto, ON: Author. Retrieved from http://www.edu.gov.on.ca/eng/document/reports/OME_Report09_EN.pdf

Curran, Ruth, Balfanz, Robert, & Herzog, Liza. (2007, October). An early warning system. *Educational Leadership, 65*(2), 28–33.

Devaney, L. (2009, November 3). Educators focus on dropout prevention. *eSchool News.* Retrieved from https://www.eschoolnews.com/2009/11/03/educators-focus-on-dropout-prevention

Education Quality and Accountability Office (EQAO). (2010, December). *Program for International Student Assessment (PISA), 2009 highlights of Ontario student results.* Toronto, ON: Author. Retrieved from http://www.eqao.com/pdf_e/10/2009_PISA_Highlights_en.pdf

Education Quality and Accountability Office (EQAO). (2011). *Highlights of the provincial achievement results.* Toronto, ON: Author. Retrieved from http://www.eqao.com/pdf_e/11/EQAO_PJ9Highlights_2011.pdf

Hale, J. (2004, November). How schools shortchange African American children. *Educational Leadership, 62*(3), 34–37.

King, A. J. C. (2004, January). *Double cohort study: Phase 3 report.* Toronto: Ontario Ministry of Education.

Levin, B. (2003). "Approaches to Equity in Policy for Lifelong Learning." Paris: Education and Training Policy Division, OECD.

Levin, H. M. (2011, February). *Why should countries care: The high economic and social costs of education failure* [PowerPoint slides]. Retrieved from http://www.oecd.org/edu/preschoolandschool/45158221.pdf

McKinsey & Company (2009, April). *The economic impact of the achievement gap in America's schools.* New York: McKinsey & Company, Social Sector Office. Retrieved from https://mckinseyonsociety.com/downloads/reports/Education/achievement_gap_report.pdf

Ontario Ministry of Education. (2009). *Realizing the promise of diversity: Ontario's equity and inclusive education strategy.* Toronto: Queen's Printer for Ontario.

2

Excellence and Equity

The future well-being of all countries is dependent on ensuring excellence in education and equity of outcomes for all students. Leaders from business, industry, and labor, as well as policy makers and parents, are asking their governments to ensure increasing success for all students, regardless of background or personal circumstances. Demands for greater accountability in investments in education are reverberating as politicians make promises to constituents to provide value for money and to bring about change with a sense of urgency. There is an expectation that school systems will achieve both excellence and equity and will ensure that more students graduate from high school.

Excellence and Equity

Achieving excellence and equity requires that educators raise the bar and close achievement gaps. There must be discernible improvement for all groups along the achievement spectrum. It means that schools are expected to create the conditions for success for all students, especially those who have not seen success in large numbers in the past. This includes groups such as students in special education programs, immigrants, boys, and students living in poverty. The primary intent is to ensure that schools help students overcome any barriers or limitations placed on them by virtue of background factors.

One of the ways to determine if we have an equitable system is to disaggregate achievement data along demographic and other lines that divide people in society. The notion is that intelligence exists in all groups. If, indeed, we believe that all children can learn and achieve with proper supports, then it is our responsibility as educators to ensure that students from all backgrounds are represented along the continuum. If any group is clustered at the bottom of the achievement ladder, it is evidence enough that the system is not an equitable one. One of the primary purposes of schools is to ensure success for all students.

One of the most popular discussions today is that a good education includes what are being described as 21st century skills. Wagner (2008) refers to some of these skills as *survival skills*. He advocates strongly for the schooling that students will need if they are to be prepared to function in a global economy. This schooling would focus on the following skills:

1. Critical thinking and problem solving

2. Collaboration and leadership

3. Agility and adaptability

4. Initiative and entrepreneurialism

5. Effective oral and written communication

6. Accessing and analyzing information

7. Curiosity and imagination

The 21st century learning movement has gained momentum in recent years. There are some individuals, including educators, who believe that schools have always taught these skills, which can be found in one form or another in curriculum documents written over the last 15 years. Others will admit that, at best, they are platitudinous statements that have never been made concrete or resulted in practical and relevant skill-development initiatives. In any event, these skills are back on the agenda with extensive support that they should be taught in a systematic and intentional manner to prepare students to compete in the global community.

Sternberg (2008) posits that the way we define excellence determines our path toward achieving it. He discusses four models of excellence and concludes that excellence means achieving above average. Valiga (2010) asserts that excellence is a habit or way of life, a process. It involves challenging ourselves to do things beyond what we have mastered. It also means having a growth orientation.

For us, excellence is about constantly pushing the boundaries to reach higher—stretching oneself to achieve ever-moving targets and soaring to the zenith of possibilities. It is about doing one's personal best and having a strong belief that only the best is good enough. It is about what grandparents would have said many years ago when lamps were in vogue and electricity was not in widespread use. Those who strive for excellence were willing to "burn the midnight oil."

VanTassel-Baska (1997) approaches excellence from the vantage point of the individual's habits of mind, as well as the process of working toward an ideal standard and attaining a consistently high standard of performance in an endeavor that is socially valued and accepted.

There are still some educators who see equity and excellence as polar opposites and who claim that they cannot be pursued or achieved simultaneously. Our experience tells us that they must both co-exist. If, for example, a school system is to be described as excellent, it means that all students are achieving at their highest potential. The notion of raising the bar and closing the gaps is the excellence that equity requires. VanTassel-Baska (1997) agrees that these concepts are both necessary and must be held in "creative tension." At the very least, we see these as complementary approaches.

Gross (1989) equates excellence with the need to achieve success and the motivation to learn at high levels. Gardner (1961) defines excellence as striving for quality in all areas of a society. Roeper (1996) views excellence as a standard for gifted students to achieve in psychic terms, learning to develop as ethical and moral human beings.

Silverman (1993) maintains that excellence cannot be defined solely as *success* because our culture refuses to recognize the contributions of many disenfranchised groups, particularly women, who attain excellence in areas like homemaking and childrearing. Thus, excellence may be conceived of as a synonym for success, achievement, or psychic growth, depending on one's definitional structure.

There are three seminal writers in the field of equity in terms of their discussion of what is described as culturally responsive pedagogy. They are Gay (1990), Asante (1991), and Hilliard (2008). It is the perspective of Gay that, for students to be successful, curriculum must be pluralistic in its content and methodology. Teaching is a socio-cultural process in which success for culturally different students requires certain skills and awareness on the part of the teacher.

These skills include the conceptualization of equity in terms of comparability or equivalence of learning opportunities for diverse learners instead of as the same treatment for everyone. Gay (1990) seeks to encourage teachers to become aware of their routine teaching behaviors, which militate against educational equity, and to modify instructional procedures to accommodate cultural differences. She emphasizes that knowing how to differentiate instruction to make high-status knowledge accessible to all students is the essence of equity. Certain types of knowledge should not be the sole province of students who are fast learners. Teaching with equity means that all students must gain fluency in their ways of knowing, studying, asking, answering and understanding, cogitating, expressing, and engaging others. Furthermore, it means helping students from diverse backgrounds to broaden their repertoires of learning strategies and skills.

One of Gay's (1990) most important contributions to the understanding of equity is her caution against confusing educational means with educational ends. We are not to equate the differentiating of instructional methods with the lowering of educational standards—a stance often taken by individuals who are not yet convinced that differentiation is essential in the teaching and learning process. Equity and excellence, far from being polar opposites, she observed, are inextricably intertwined. In fact, they are two sides of the same coin.

Hilliard (2008), who also wrote extensively on the topic of culturally responsive pedagogy, stated that if curriculum is centered in truth, it is pluralistic—that such a curriculum presents a truthful and meaningful rendition of the whole human experience for the simple fact that human culture is the product of the struggles of all humanity and not the province of a single racial or ethnic group. He was forceful in his conclusion that "curriculum catechism" and "cultural totalitarianism" are more associated with propaganda than with truth.

Asante (1991) says that educators must ensure curriculum equity if we are to center students in ways that make learning interesting and intimate. Centering can reduce feelings of dislocation engendered by a curriculum that does not enhance the self-esteem of students who do not belong to the dominant culture. It is Asante's view that respect is an essential component of empowerment. In turn, students feel empowered when they are part of what they create and they can relate to the information used in the classroom.

Asante (1991) observes that schools have a profoundly mono-cultural approach to information and knowledge. This worldview, he emphasizes, does not capture or grasp the attention of students of diverse background—many of whom, after some time, refuse to learn. He asserts that students must become agents rather than subjects and that it is necessary for them to develop an "organic relationship" with the subject matter. It is wrong for some children to go through school with no positive identification with their own cultures. As educators, it is important for us to continue to ensure that curriculum reflects the life experiences of our students. One may begin with illustrations, references, and examples from the students' cultural backgrounds. Congruence between the world of the student and the curriculum can increase motivation, and, in turn, can contribute to student success and retention.

The statement that the curriculum should not alienate the student must be considered when we educate in diverse settings. Often, books or knowledge that are considered to be the "classics" for dominant groups are seen as sources of pain and shame for racialized groups. Educators committed to equity may well heed the saying "Where you stand depends on where you sit."

The need to solicit the feelings of students and the impact of the curriculum on their sensibilities is an important aspect of educating for equity, diversity, and inclusion.

Characteristics of Effective Teachers in Diverse Backgrounds

Teachers who are comfortable with diversity and who often choose to work in these contexts require certain qualities to be effective. In addition to being free of biases and prejudices, they should have

- a strong belief in the ability of students to be successful,
- a belief that the skills to educate all children successfully can be learned,
- pedagogical expertise and competence,
- commitment to collaboration,
- a willingness to explore a wide range of strategies,
- a relentless focus on improvement,
- the will to persist in spite of challenges,
- a belief that excellence and equity must co-exist, and
- a conviction that teachers of all backgrounds can develop the empathy and teaching strategies necessary to teach students from diverse backgrounds successfully and to make a difference in their lives

The Global Preoccupation With Increasing Graduation Rates

Internationally, one of the most popular goals of governments is to increase graduation rates. A good education and an educated populace are linked to economic stability, national prosperity, and social well-being, among other benefits. Parents want their children to be better educated than they were. Governments want a more educated workforce. Society, in general, wants a more educated citizenry in the quest to sustain democracy. Raising the level of education by improving graduation rates has become an international preoccupation. With that goes the clarion call to educators to work with students who need support to make it to the finishing line.

Numerous reports have shown that the investment in education improves psychological, social, and economic conditions, not just for individuals but also for society as a whole (e.g., Wilkinson & Pickett, 2009). Additionally, research has shown that the challenge to improve education outcomes is achievable in a relatively short time. We now know that we can, through targeted interventions and innovative strategies, raise the bar for all students and close the achievement gaps once thought to be insuperable. The success of the Ontario improvement strategy is one case in point.

International Comparisons

Internationally, there are many educational systems that are realizing great success in improving achievement for all students. Barber and Mourshed (2007) studied 25 of the world's school systems, including 10 of the highest performing. Based on comparative assessments of student achievement on these international tests, Ontario was ranked as one of the top 10 high-performing school systems in the world. They examined characteristics that these top performers had in common and strategies they used to improve student achievement. They found three key factors:

1. Getting the right people to become teachers

2. Developing them into effective instructors

3. Ensuring the system is available to deliver the best possible instruction for every child

As well, they identified the following lessons learned:

Lesson 1: The quality of an educational system cannot exceed the quality of its teachers.

Lesson 2: The only way to improve outcomes is to improve instruction.

Lesson 3:   High performance requires every student to succeed.

Lesson 4:   Great leadership at the school level is a key enabling factor.

In 2010, the researchers conducted a follow-up study, which showed that Ontario, along with four other jurisdictions (Singapore, Hong Kong, South Korea, and Saxony, Germany), was able to sustain the gains it had made to further improve student success (Mourshed, Chijioke, & Barber, 2010). Ontario was identified as a "great system." According to OECD, as well, Ontario is considered across the world as one of the fastest-improving systems. What makes Ontario such an exciting international example is that, not too long ago, it was considered by many to be a system in crisis. Now, it is seen as one of the few jurisdictions that continue to demonstrate that excellence and equity can go hand in hand.

A 2011 OECD report concluded that Canada has become a world leader in improving student achievement. The report acknowledges the strides that have been made in Ontario and commends the province's focus on capacity building and reliance on the professionalism of teachers and principals (p. 65). In addition to realizing excellence in performance, the system is given credit for achieving progress and for improved performance in spite of socioeconomic status, first language, or status as native Canadians or recent immigrants. For OECD, this shows how consistent application of centrally driven pressure for higher results, combined with extensive capacity building and a climate of relative trust and mutual respect, have enabled the Ontario system to achieve progress on key indicators.

Research clearly shows us that the highest-performing school systems are those that not only strive for excellence but are committed to equity of outcomes as well. In his research paper conducted for the UNESCO Institute of Statistics Willms (2006), points out that

> successful schools tend to be those that bolster the performance of students from less advantaged backgrounds. Similarly, countries that have the highest levels of performance tend to be those that are successful in not only raising the learning bar, but also levelling it. (p. 67)

Achieving both excellence and equity was foundational to Ontario's improvement strategy. If we are to achieve our goal of having more graduates, it is necessary to support all students, regardless of background factors, to be successful in our school systems.

The Equity Agenda

When examining school achievement data, it is evident that there are groups of students who have historically underperformed. Children whose families live in poverty, who come from minoritized backgrounds, Aboriginal students, and students who may not speak the dominant language often are overrepresented in the low-performing ranks of our schools. If we are to improve our graduation rates, we must ensure that supports are in place to give these students a hand up. In recent years, many jurisdictions across Canada and other countries have been focusing on the need to achieve equity of outcomes for students from diverse populations. The need to raise the bar for all students and to close the gap for those who are not achieving is being strongly emphasized.

Across Canada, provinces such as Alberta, Saskatchewan, Nova Scotia, Quebec, and British Columbia, for example, have identified equity goals and policies for their systems.

The Ontario Ministry of Education recently published a strategy document titled *Realizing the Promise of Diversity: Ontario's Equity and Inclusive Education Strategy* (2009). This is currently being implemented in all Ontario schools. It begins by highlighting the three core priorities of the government, asserting that the goals and intentions remain the same in the implementation of the equity strategy:

- High levels of student achievement
- Reduced gaps in student achievement
- Increased public confidence in publicly funded education

The strategy affirms the belief of Canadians in multiculturalism, human rights, and diversity as fundamental values while acknowledging that racism, homophobia, sexism, and other anti-human values still exist. It specifically mentions cyberbullying, hate propaganda on the Internet, and homophobia as issues of major concerns to parents and students alike. In recent years, there have been documented incidents of bullying, anti-black racism, anti-Semitism, and Islamophobia. Whereas these acts are by no means pervasive, the issue is that when students attend school, they have a right to be free of harassment, violence, and malice in speech or action, and that schools have an obligation to provide a positive learning environment for all students and staffs. This reassurance is necessary given the diversity that currently exists in schools. Students who feel marginalized in any way need support to do well and to perform at their best.

The commitment to equity and diversity provides a strong statement of belief in Ontario's diversity as one of its greatest assets.

Respecting and valuing the range of differences that exists in this society is one way of realizing the promise of diversity. Likewise, the centrality of an equitable and inclusive education in creating a cohesive society and a strong economy helps to ensure and secure the future prosperity of the province. This is an important focus of Ontario's equity strategy.

The vision for equity paints a compelling picture of an inclusive education system in which all students, parents, and other members of the school community are welcomed and respected, and every student is supported and inspired to succeed in a culture of high expectations for learning.

The guiding principles for Ontario's equity strategy indicate that an equitable and inclusive education

- is a foundation of excellence,
- meets individual needs,
- identifies and eliminates barriers,
- promotes a sense of belonging,
- involves the broad community,
- builds on and enhances previous and existing initiatives, and
- is demonstrated throughout the system.

Ontario has set out clear goals and timelines for all school districts to follow in implementing the expectations of the provincial strategy. The Ministry of Education has provided guidance, support, and professional learning opportunities to assist with the implementation process. Each district is expected to have a clear equity policy with a lead person appointed to ensure implementation. Schools are required to ensure a safe, supportive, positive, and inclusive environment that strengthens equity and diversity.

The concrete actions that have resulted from the equity policy and the requirement that districts report to the Ministry of Education on the progress of this strategy in the annual report of the director of education (chief superintendent) provide a clear signal that the Ministry takes this strategy very seriously.

What are some of the indicators of an equitable school? A few jurisdictions have developed their own documents to assist in the identification of these indicators. The York Region District School Board in Toronto, for example, has worked on this issue over many years and has several documents on its website related to equity issues. Please refer to www.yrdsb.edu.on.ca for policies, programs, and documents, one of which addresses specifically the notion of ensuring student success by identifying antiracist indicators for an antiracist school.

The following are a few of the indicators that will help to determine if equity is being taken seriously in a school or district:

- High expectations for achievement are communicated to and expected of students and staff.
- Curriculum materials are reviewed continuously for biases such as those related to race, gender, socioeconomic status, and other grounds included in human rights codes.
- Curriculum resources, subject content, and textbooks are selected for inclusiveness, relevance, and applicability to the lives of students and are screened to avoid bias.
- The curriculum is user-friendly and does not exclude or alienate students.
- Classroom instruction is culturally responsive to the diverse school population.
- The school staff members are reflective of the larger community.
- The staff members are able to recognize and deal with prejudice in themselves and in students.
- The staff address systemic barriers that limit the life chances of students.
- The teaching and classroom practices are free of bias.
- Achievement data are disaggregated by race, gender, socioeconomic status, and other variables to ascertain specific student needs.
- Students see themselves and their cultural backgrounds reflected in the curriculum.
- Zero tolerance for racism and other human rights issues is clearly articulated.
- Parents feel welcome in the school and are encouraged to play a meaningful role in their children's education.
- Cultural and class biases in standardized tests are recognized and are not used as a basis for decision making about program selection and placement of students.
- To an outsider, placement in programs (such as special education) and learning groups would not appear to be based on race, gender, or social class.
- Students are demitted regularly from special education programs.
- The culture and management of the school are bias free.
- Discipline is applied consistently and fairly.
- Those who graduate from the school reflect the race, gender, and socioeconomic diversity that exists in the school.

Too often, students who are at risk of dropping out of school do not feel that they are valued members of the school community. They often do not see themselves in the curriculum or recognize the relevance of material studied. When conducting research factors that cause students to drop out of school, Ferguson, Tilleczek, Boydell, and Anneke Rummens (2005) identified the main risk factors for youth from visible minorities dropping out of school. These factors included the following:

- Exposure to stereotypes and prejudice in school
- Streaming, or being "forced out" of the regular school program
- Difficult interactions with school administrators
- Higher rates of detentions, suspensions, and retentions
- Unfair and/or ineffective discipline
- Nonrelevant curriculum
- Low academic involvement
- Low familial educational levels
- Limited support for remaining in school
- Early assumption of adult roles

While the school cannot control all of these factors, it is evident that much can be done at the school level to help mitigate these issues.

We must realize that if the status quo is not working for all of our students, it is up to all educators to make changes in current policy, practices, and behaviors that will help all of our students to be successful. We need to make all students and their families feel welcome and valued in our schools. We need to reflect honestly on our own biases and attitudes to ensure our expectations for certain groups of students are not negatively influenced. Schools control many of the conditions for the success of our students, and it is through our collective efforts that we help students increase their life choices and chances. Helping all students graduate from high school opens many doors for a brighter future.

References

Asante, M. K. (1991). The Afrocentric idea in education. *The Journal of Negro Education, 60*(2), 170–180.

Barber, M., & Mourshed, M. (2007). *How the world's best-performing school systems come out on top.* London: McKinsey & Company.

Ferguson, B., Tilleczek, K., Boydell, K., & Anneke Rummens, K. (2005). *Early school leavers: Understanding the lived reality of student disengagement from secondary school: Final report.* Toronto: Ontario Ministry of Education.

Gay, G. (1990). Achieving educational equality through curriculum desegregation. *Phi Delta Kappan, 72*(1), 56–62.

Gardner, J. (1961). *Excellence: Can we be equal and excellent too?* New York: Harper.

Gross, M. U. M. (1989). The pursuit of excellence or the search for intimacy? The forced-choice dilemma of gifted youth. *Roeper Review, 11*(4), 189–194.

Hilliard, A. G., III (1991). Why we must pluralize the curriculum. *Educational Leadership, 49*(4), 12–16.

Mourshed, M., Chijioke, C., & Barber, M. (2010). *How the world's most improved school systems keep getting better.* New York: McKinsey Company.

Ontario Ministry of Education. (2009). *Realizing the promise of diversity: Ontario's equity and inclusive education policy.* Toronto: Author.

Organisation for Economic Co-operation and Development (OECD). (2011). *Lessons from PISA for the United States.* Paris: Author.

Roeper, A. (1996). A personal statement of philosophy of George & Annemarie Roeper. *Roeper Review, 19*(1), 18–19.

Royal Commission on Learning. (1994). *For the love of learning: Report of the Royal Commission on Learning.* Toronto: Publications Ontario.

Silverman, L. (1993). *Counseling the gifted and talented.* Denver, CO: Love Publishing Company.

Sternberg, R. (2008). Excellence for all. *Educational Leadership, 66*(2), 14–19.

Valiga, T. M. (2010). Excellence—does the word mean anything anymore? *Journal of Nursing Education, 49*(8), 427–428.

VanTassel-Baska, J. (1997). Excellence as a standard for all education. *Roeper Review, 20*(1), 9–13.

Wagner, T. (2008). Rigour redefined. *Educational Leadership, 66*(2), 20–25.

Wilkinson, R., & Pickett, K. (2009). *The spirit level: Why equality is better for everyone.* London: Penguin Books.

Willms, D. (2006). *Learning divides: Ten policy questions about the performance and equity of schools and school systems.* Montreal, PQ: UNESCO Institute for Statistics.

3

District and School Improvement

A Blueprint for Success

Effective school districts and schools are those that focus on continuous improvement. They regularly reflect on their practice and identify what is working and what is not. They determine the greatest area of need for their students and then collaboratively develop an improvement process to meet those needs. To improve graduation rates, schools should reflect continuously on their practice and make changes where necessary to ensure that all students are making progress toward achieving their graduation requirements.

Improvement is possible in every school. With focused attention and deep implementation of effective strategies, schools can improve and reach high levels of student achievement. Planning for improvement must be a cyclical and continuous process. It involves evaluating the current status, identifying a few precise goals, implementing research-informed strategies to achieve the goals, and monitoring progress. Too often, when districts and schools engage in the development of an improvement plan, they try to do too much, and the reality is that not much actually gets done. When improvement plans try to be everything to everybody, they become unmanageable and often are too vague. Deep implementation of a small number of precise goals greatly surpasses the shallow implementation of many goals. As Ben Levin (2008), former deputy minister of education in Ontario, points out, "No organization can do everything at once at a high level, and successful large-scale improvement requires identifying and focussing relentlessly on a small number of high profile priorities which are most likely to improve student achievement" (p. 201).

The key to improvement is the implementation of effective processes that involve a whole district and school effort. The purpose of any improvement plan is that it results in action in the school and classroom, resulting in improved student learning. It is not sufficient to just develop the plan; even more important is to have an effective implementation process and a vehicle for monitoring progress. All too often, improvement efforts are too vague and do not involve those responsible for implementation. This chapter provides guidance for district and school leaders on how to develop a collaborative improvement process to ensure student achievement gains.

Consistency and Focus

The study of Mourshed, Chijioke, and Barber, titled *How the World's Most Improved School Systems Keep Getting Better* (2010), suggests that by prescribing adequacy, an educational system can unleash greatness. By this statement, the authors are suggesting that a consistent minimum expectation, clearly articulated and supported, can provide the foundation for collaborative work that fosters the individual and collective creativity on which meaningful change so often depends. One such example of such prescribed adequacy has been the focus on and support of improvement planning processes in Ontario. As Ontario launched its reform initiative, all district school boards and schools were expected to conduct a self-assessment and to develop and implement improvement plans. The Ontario Ministry of Education provided districts and schools with a range of supports to assist with the improvement process. As a result, Ontario has managed to achieve significant gains in student achievement and has become one of five international systems identified as being on the journey from "great to excellent" (p. 19).

To effectively support the improvement of Ontario's education system, it was important to provide some common frameworks within which school districts could work to become more informed, precise, and strategic in targeting areas for sustained improvement in student achievement. Once such frameworks were in place, a system to support the implementation of the improvement plans and the effective monitoring of that improvement was necessary. A fine balance for improvement was necessary, wherein the research-informed framework could be used, but in which the individual needs and strengths of the districts could be reflected in a differentiated model that engaged each district in the self-improvement process.

Achieving Continuous Improvement

Plan

- Establish an improvement team that is representative of the entire organization and will lead the improvement process.
- Conduct a needs assessment by gathering and analyzing current data.
- Engage all staff in a collaborative process to review findings and establish priorities or goals.
- Focus on outcomes for students.
- Develop SMART goals that include ambitious targets.
- Identify research-informed strategies that everyone will implement to achieve goals.
- Determine resources and professional development that will be needed.
- Develop monitoring strategies.

Act/Implement

- Implement strategies to achieve goals.
- Purchase or acquire necessary resources.
- Communicate goals and timelines to all stakeholders.
- Provide ongoing professional learning to support implementation.

Observe/Monitor

- Gather data at the onset of the cycle.
- Monitor progress regularly.
- Bring evidence of progress regularly to staff meetings.
- Share samples of student work to demonstrate progress toward goals.
- Ask staff to share successful practice.
- Encourage staff to share challenges and solve issues collaboratively.

Reflect and Assess

- Evaluate the effectiveness of the plan.
- Identify lessons learned and next steps.

Keys to Improvement

The three main keys to system improvement are planning, implementation, and monitoring. The Ontario journey has been one characterized by action research and collaborative inquiry wherein districts and the Ministry staff learned together how current research should best be applied and which strategies were most effective within the context of a given educational unit (school, classroom, division, department, or district). An emphasis on improvement planning and effective processes was foundational to Ontario's success. The strategies that resulted in steady progress in student achievement are grounded in international research and have application in jurisdictions beyond Ontario.

Figure 3.1 provides an overview of the improvement planning cycle.

Figure 3.1   Improvement Planning Cycle

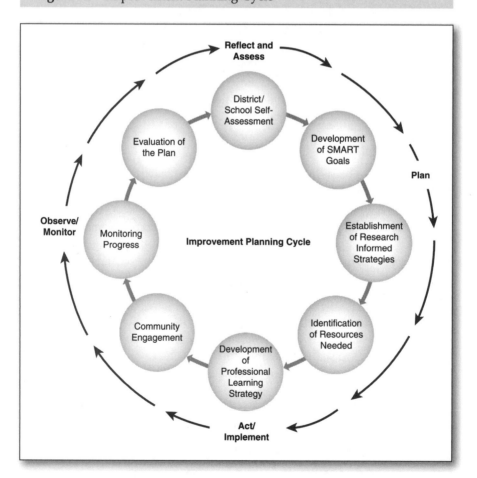

Developing the Plan for Continuous Improvement

In developing the improvement strategy for Ontario, the province learned from the successes and failures in other jurisdictions around the globe, from current research, and from the extensive efforts of the province's school districts over the preceding 8 years as they had addressed the issue of improvement in their districts. School districts and schools in Ontario were invited to submit their district and school improvement plans to the Ministry for analysis. It was through this analysis, which involved 72 district improvement plans and over 200 school plans, that the Ministry was able to determine strengths and challenges in the improvement process. What was discovered through this process was that there was great variability in how boards and schools viewed the improvement planning process. Not surprisingly, the boards and schools that were achieving continuous improvement shared some common characteristics in their planning process. These included

- an improvement team to guide the process,
- a collaborative and inclusive improvement process,
- an ongoing district/school assessment tool to determine the greatest area of need for students,
- the identification of a small number of precise (SMART) goals,
- the establishment of ambitious targets based on both external standards and internal measures,
- the identification of research-informed strategies,
- a focus on equity of outcomes,
- identification of required resources,
- a commitment to meeting professional learning needs,
- a system for monitoring progress with specific timelines,
- a willingness to revise the plan as needed
- a formal evaluation of the effectiveness of the plan, and
- identification of lessons learned.

In all of these schools and districts, the improvement process was collaborative, involving all stakeholders. It was clear that educators in these districts did not settle for the status quo; they were focused on continuous improvement. They used their data to narrow their improvement focus and set priorities. To determine a small number of SMART goals, staff conducted a needs assessment to determine the area of greatest need for students.

SMART Goals

Developing precise SMART (specific, measurable, attainable, results-based, and time-bound) goals is critical to moving a school or system forward. The goals should have a focus on outcomes—that is, what students will do differently once the goal has been attained— and are measured using the same data and evidence that were used to identify the learning need initially. Appendix 1 provides a template for reflective questions that can be used with staff when developing SMART goals.

Ontario, like many jurisdictions, has a process to assess student performance. These tests in reading, writing, and mathematics are administered in Grades 3 and 6, and in Grade 9 for mathematics. Finally, a test of literacy (Ontario sets the standard at a Grade 9 level of reading and writing as a graduation requirement) is administered in Grade 10. These achievement data, in addition to diagnostic and class-room assessments, are used as the basis for setting precise goals. It is very important that the goals and the strategies intended to bring them about be focused on actions that may be measured in the school year and not based solely on year-end and standardized testing results. This matters because if the key measurement of student progress is not made until after the school year has finished, there can be no in-cycle adaptation. As well, there will be no real sense of whether the strategies are working or not within a time frame that allows for improvements and modifications to be made in time to benefit the students.

As goals were identified, district and school teams focused on the critical few areas rather than the superficial many. An effective plan usually contains no more than two or three SMART goals. Ambitious targets were set within the SMART goals, and baseline data were identified.

Target Setting

A powerful strategy that was used in Ontario when working toward improvement goals was the establishment of ambitious but attainable achievement targets. Every district and school in the province was required to establish targets for improving student achievement. The targets were specified within the districts' SMART goals. Staff from the Ministry of Education reviewed the targets with all districts and assisted them in revising targets that were not overly ambitious. Districts and schools were explicit about their achievement targets and the timeline for meeting their goals. Progress in meeting targets was monitored regularly. If progress was not being made, then Ministry staff worked with districts and schools to revise current improvement strategies. The province not only expected districts and schools to establish targets but also lead the way by establishing provincial targets for Grade 6 reading, writing, and mathematics and for graduation rates.

It is important to view target setting not as a prediction based on past performance but rather as a commitment to reach a stated goal that will lead to improvement. When setting targets, improvement teams should review achievement data and other relevant information to determine gaps between the current state and the desired goals of student achievement. Targets are like road signs that help us measure our progress along our improvement journey. Ensuring that all districts and boards establish achievement targets provided a clear focus for improvement in Ontario. The key aspect of the target-setting process was that specific targets were not imposed on districts or schools by the province. Districts and schools set their own targets based on their current attainment levels in consultation with Ministry staff.

Through careful analysis of trends in achievement data, targets can be set to provide a focus for improvement efforts. By establishing clear targets, it is evident that the organization is committed to improvement. Targets should clearly articulate the number or percentage of students who will meet specific achievement goals by a given point in time. It is important that targets are developed collaboratively with staff, discussed openly, and monitored regularly.

Collaboration Is Essential

In districts and schools that were improving student achievement, staff worked collaboratively to identify a small number of research-informed strategies that they felt would have the greatest impact in achieving their SMART goals and achievement targets. By working together, they were able to use the collective expertise and knowledge of the staff to identify strategies that research supported and that their experience showed would work. In these schools and districts, equity of outcomes was a central part of the discussion; the goal was not just to raise the bar in student achievement but also to close gaps between students.

Timelines for the implementation of improvement strategies and monitoring strategies were clearly identified. Establishing frequent checkpoints to determine progress in achieving goals enabled staff to make mid-course corrections in the plan as needed.

The responsibility for monitoring progress was shared among all staff. They identified specific points in time when they would evaluate the plan to determine lessons learned—what worked well, what didn't, and why.

To achieve continuous improvement, educators must commit to meeting regularly to reflect on their practice, examine achievement data, raise questions, and collaboratively problem solve collaboratively. There is a great deal of collective wisdom, knowledge, and experience within districts and schools. The secret to continuous improvement is to tap that collective talent. District and school administrators should work with their staff to build professional learning communities that take collective responsibility for continuous improvement. As Schmoker (2005) points out,

> If there is anything that the research community agrees on, it is this: The right kind of continuous, structured teacher collaboration improves the quality of teaching and pays big, often immediate dividends in student learning and professional morale in virtually any setting. (p. xii)

Finding ways to engage staff in the improvement process is essential if districts and schools are to meet with success. Throughout this chapter, a number of strategies are shared that will promote a collaborative approach to district and school improvement.

Effective improvement processes facilitate the involvement of parents and the school community. Parents and community members can provide valuable insights into their perception of strengths and areas in need of improvement. Through town hall meetings, surveys, and information evenings, districts and schools can gather valuable data. Communicating the improvement plan and providing regular updates in progress can be a powerful tool to gain support and strengthen the credibility of the district or school.

Effective Improvement Plans

From our analysis of Ontario district and school improvement plans, it was clear that there was some confusion about what constituted a good improvement planning process. In many cases, boards and schools simply listed all of the things they were currently doing, rather than just focusing on the greatest area in need of improvement. Frequently, we saw goals that were not specific, plans with too many initiatives, a lack of evidence that a comprehensive analysis of available data was occurring, or little or no attention to monitoring processes.

It is a fallacy to think that if something is not in the school improvement plan, then it is not important. Having a specific focus for improvement does not mean that this is all we care about. It means that this is what we are focusing our improvement efforts on at this particular point in time. Improvement plans should focus on the most urgent learning needs of our students as priorities. Finding

> ### What an Improvement Plan Is Not . . .
>
> - Not an annual report
> - Not a narrative of everything currently being done
> - Not a list of events
> - Not a static document
> - Not a document that the principal develops in isolation
>
> An improvement plan should focus only on those things that we intend to improve or refine, not on everything that we are already doing.

the focus for improvement plans means identifying the critical few things we need to pay attention to at this particular time. The focus is not forever; it lasts only until we achieve our goal, and then we move on to another area of need. It is important for schools and districts not to lose sight of the successful practices that have brought them to their current level while maintaining their focus on continuous improvement.

Components of Effective Plans

Effective improvement plans share some common components:

- ☐ A district or school self-assessment, which includes an analysis of school data (e.g., student assignments, school grading reports, diagnostic assessments, external state/provincial assessments, disciplinary records, attendance records, graduation rates, etc.)
- ☐ A small number of SMART goals
- ☐ A manageable number of research-informed strategies that will be implemented to achieve the goals
- ☐ Targeted resources
- ☐ Professional learning requirements
- ☐ Strategies to engage parents/community
- ☐ Monitoring strategies and timelines
- ☐ Measures of progress in achieving goals
- ☐ Overall evaluation of the plan
- ☐ Lessons learned and next steps

Appendix 2 provides a sample template for developing improvement plans.

It is critical to the success of the improvement plan that key stakeholders have a role in its development. Districts and schools should develop an improvement team to guide the improvement process. The team should have representation from a wide range of stakeholders. Everyone involved in the implementation of the plan should have an opportunity for input. By involving staff in the examination of school data through a school self-assessment, questions begin to arise:

- In what areas are our students most successful? How do we know?
- In what areas of the curriculum do our students have difficulties?
- Who are the students who are struggling?
- What are some possible causes for their difficulties?
- What are the greatest areas of need for our students?

By engaging staff in such discussions, the focus for improvement can be narrowed and improvement goals be established. Appendix 3 provides some key questions to support improvement planning at the district level, while Appendix 4 and 5 provide sample improvement plan checklists.

There are four key processes in the improvement cycle: observe, reflect, plan, and act. In the observation stage, the process calls for the analysis of evidence in a self-assessment process. The reflection on those observations is manifested by the development of SMART goals that are student focused and intended to address the greatest area of need as identified through a self-assessment of the district or school. The planning phase considers the explicit and research/evidence-informed strategies that will be implemented to attain the goals developed. Also in the planning phase is the consideration of what resources will be developed and allocated to support the strategies created. Determining who will be responsible for various aspects of implementation of the plan is vital. Finally, a professional learning strategy, aimed at building the capacity of educators to deliver the strategies and achieve the goals, should be developed. Ongoing reflection is essential so that staff can review the progress being made, evaluate the effectiveness of the plan, and make revisions where needed if progress is not being made.

Self-Assessment

Any improvement endeavor must be grounded in the common understanding that there are issues that require improvement. In education, these issues are most commonly some measure of student achievement, leading us to conclude that some students are not achieving at appropriate levels. Therefore, it is necessary that educational systems—be they classrooms, divisions or departments, schools, regions, districts, or an entire province, state, or nation—engage in open, honest, and evidence-informed self-assessment of the metrics by which they measure success and of the processes, practices, and strategies by which they currently seek to leverage changes in learning.

To improve student achievement, schools can engage in a collaborative self-assessment process to determine what is working well, and areas in need of attention and further development. Self-assessment enables an organization to get to know itself better, identify priorities for improvement, and leverage change. Research has shown that there are a number of factors that correlate school effectiveness to improved student achievement (Lezotte, 2005; Marzano, 2003). The question we should ask ourselves is whether those factors are in place in our districts and schools.

Ontario developed a number of tools to assist school districts in conducting an assessment and structure a plan for improvement. This allowed for each district's individual needs, strengths, and characteristics to be reflected, while also establishing a common framework to measure effectiveness. The K–12 Improvement Planning Assessment Tool (for more information about this tool, see http://www.edu.gov .on.ca/eng/policyfunding/memos/september2012/ImprovePlan AssessTool.pdf) first directs districts to consider a broad scope of evidence as an indication of where issues of student learning need to be addressed. The tool outlines potential sources of data and questions that districts can consider with respect to student achievement data, demographic data, program data, and perceptual data. Guiding questions for data analysis provide prompts that assist teams in making sense of the ample data sources that are available to them. This common framework, the "prescribed adequacy" of Mourshed et al. (2010) report, allows the creativity and differentiated strategies of each district to "unleash greatness" and contribute to the overall improvement of student outcomes as they move through the remaining stages of the improvement cycle.

Ontario realized that continuous improvement could not be attained through top-down measures and edicts for change. For true reform to take hold, educators needed to be given the opportunity to take responsibility for professional accountability. To that end, the Ministry of Education constructed a tool for boards and schools to use to measure their own effectiveness. This tool is known in Ontario as the School Effectiveness Framework (SEF). Additional information about SEF can

be found on the Ontario Ministry of Education website: www.edu.gov
.on.ca; see also Ontario Ministry of Education, 2010. When creating this
framework, the Ministry looked for successful practices within the
province and internationally, as well as examining current research by
leaders in the field.

Ontario is not alone in its commitment to self-assessment. In the
United Kingdom, Ofsted (2006) has stated that self-evaluation is becoming more important in the work of schools, colleges, and local authorities. In 2009, the Australia Capital Territory Department of Education
and Training published *The School Improvement Framework*, which outlines processes for self-assessment, planning, external validation, and
reporting that enable all schools to account for their performance and
achievement in a transparent manner. The expectation is that between
2009 and 2013, all school communities will use the framework to "reflect
on the quality of their practices, identify strategic priorities, and implement effective, engaging, and challenging programs for all students" (p.
iii). Educators in many jurisdictions are finding self-assessment to be
foundational to school improvement.

The Ontario Ministry of Education's Literacy and Numeracy
Secretariat (2008) saw school self-assessment as

> a process undertaken collaboratively by the school, in which
> all staff members systematically gather and analyse evidence
> about how well their students are doing and then use this
> evidence to assess aspects of the school's performance. School
> self-assessment is forward thinking about change and
> improvement. It involves groups of teachers with their leader-
> ship team reflecting on their work together. (p. 11)

The SEF was designed to help schools and boards conduct a self-
assessment based on the key components that make schools effective. The tool was not used to evaluate schools, but rather to stimulate
discussion and enable staff to focus on the areas in need of improvement. Too often, accountability measures are imposed from outside
of an organization. The SEF recognized the professionalism of district and school educators to assess their effectiveness and determine
the steps needed to improve. The focused discussions that that took
place because of school self-assessments resulted in more precise
improvement planning and a shared understanding of what
makes schools effective. The Ontario philosophy respected the professionalism of educators and believed in their desire to bring about
improvement from within the profession.

The key purposes of the framework were to

- build board and school capacity in identifying strengths, areas that require attention, and next steps;
- foster introspection, reflection, and analysis;
- lead to better improvement planning with precision and intentionality;
- act as a catalyst for collaborative and collegial conversations about improvement from within;
- implement high-impact, research-informed strategies;
- determine the monitoring and feedback strategies necessary for improvement and accountability;
- provide a forum for consensus building around school improvement;
- develop a deeper understanding of the unique improvement needs of the school; and
- communicate, celebrate, and continue to build public confidence around school effectiveness.

The SEF, which was first developed as an elementary school tool and later expanded to serve secondary schools, focuses on six key areas for effective practice:

- School and classroom leadership
- Assessment for, as, and of learning
- Curriculum, teaching, and learning
- Programs and pathways
- Home, school, and community partnerships
- Student voice

The SEF provides evidenced-based indicators of successful practice in each of the above areas with potential examples of evidence that the indicator has been implemented. School leaders use the framework to conduct a self-assessment. Working as a team, they look for evidence within their school that the indicators are present. It assists schools in becoming more precise and intentional in their improvement efforts. By engaging in deep conversations, school staff are able to take collaborative action to improve identified areas.

Ministry of Education staff worked with educators across Ontario as they conducted, in many cases, what was their first school self-assessment using the SEF. The response was overwhelmingly positive. Teachers told us that when the whole staff engaged in the self-assessment, they felt empowered. They felt that their professional opinions mattered and that they were helping to shape the future direction of their school. The school staff felt that they were being more proactive in monitoring their own effectiveness. Decisions regarding school improvement were made in a more democratic fashion. There was greater sharing of information and a raised awareness of areas of concern. The teachers told us that through the process, they learned from their colleagues and improved their own practice. It was felt that the level of professionalism in the school was enhanced. Educators reported that participating in a school self-assessment was a powerful means of professional development. They said that the experience

- enhanced their self-knowledge,
- facilitated self-reflection,
- helped them to understand the school better,
- highlighted the good things they were doing,
- celebrated achievements to date,
- emphasized the impact of good teaching,
- built a sense of collective accountability,
- facilitated authentic collaboration in the development of the school improvement plan, and
- provided valuable data to inform improvement efforts.

To achieve continuous improvement, it is beneficial for schools to conduct a self-assessment to determine what is working well and the areas in need of improvement. It is just as important to acknowledge and celebrate strategies that are working as it is to identify areas of challenge. After all, if you can't articulate it, you can't sustain it. Effective schools are reflective schools.

Implementation

It is not sufficient to just develop the improvement plan; effective plans require a strong implementation process and a vehicle for monitoring progress. In the process thus far described, the key to implementation is the set of strategies and resources developed under each SMART goal. The engagement of staff in the planning process, so that they fully comprehend the nature of the needs assessment findings and why the strategies selected have been chosen, is essential to success. The vision for the plan must be clearly articulated. The more deeply it is understood, the greater the chance that it will be implemented successfully.

In organizations where change initiatives fail, it is usually because of inconsistent or superficial implementation. In districts and schools, we have often seen what appeared to be great ideas flounder because people did not pay enough attention to the hard work of implementing them. District and school leaders must make sure that the strategies in the improvement plan are implemented consistently and effectively by everyone involved. Benjamin (2011) points out, "The two most important reasons why employees fail to implement a strategy are unclear expectations and failure of the leaders to check for satisfactory implementation" (p. 27). It is important for those responsible for the improvement process to provide ongoing support to staff and to give them the opportunity to discuss implementation successes and challenges.

Key to the success of implementation is that educators are provided with opportunities to improve the knowledge and skills they will need for deep implementation. Offering ongoing professional learning provides the support needed for staff to implement improvement strategies. Current literature has shown that a collaborative professional learning community is necessary for improvement.

An effective implementation strategy identifies a lead person who, together with the team, articulates a clear plan, builds a collaborative culture, provides ongoing professional learning, identifies indicators of progress, monitors progress closely, and communicates regularly with all those involved. It is not uncommon for school improvement efforts to fail when there is a lack of communication. Those who are intimately involved and leading the process sometimes forget to keep others abreast of progress. A fear of the unknown can cause people to quietly sabotage change efforts.

When improvement efforts flounder, it is often because those responsible for the implementation do not see the need for change or have not had any input into the process. Building a school or district improvement plan is a collective activity that should involve many people from across the organization. People need to feel that they have a stake in the initiative and in its outcome. A keystone of effective implementation is to build a team of people who work together to make the change happen. Capitalizing on the collective knowledge and expertise of staff will strengthen the improvement process and facilitate deep implementation of improvement strategies.

Monitoring Progress

By establishing measurable progress indicators, systems and schools will be able to monitor progress in achieving goals in the improvement plan more easily. It is also essential to collect data regularly to assess improvement in student achievement. The results of the analysis of the data should be communicated widely so that stakeholders are aware of progress in achieving goals. If progress is evident, then the school should stay the course on the strategies it is using. If, however, the data reveal little or no progress, then the school team needs to discuss further steps that can be taken. Regular monitoring makes mid-course corrections possible.

Effective monitoring strategies identify the individuals who will take the lead in the monitoring process and clearly specify the role of everyone in the organization. Checkpoints and timelines are clearly articulated. It is critical that schools and districts establish a baseline of data, so that progress can be measured against the starting point. Everyone in the organization should be aware of the school's or district's goals, measurable targets, and ongoing progress.

It is important to keep the school or district improvement plan front and center at all times. Regular updates on progress made and discussions of challenges faced should be provided at regular staff meetings. Staff can bring samples of student work and assessments to meetings where they can collaboratively discuss whether student work is demonstrating progress in achieving achievement goals. Staff bulletins and newsletters can also provide regular updates. Providing staff with opportunities to share promising strategies that have helped move the improvement agenda forward will provide valuable professional learning opportunities. Some key questions can be asked during staff meetings to facilitate discussions about progress:

- Where were we when we started?
- Where are we now?
- Who are the students who are still struggling?
- What interventions can we provide?
- What evidence do we have that current strategies are working?
- Are there additional strategies we need to employ? If so, what are they?
- Do we have the necessary resources to facilitate continuous improvement?
- What additional professional learning do we need?
- How will we know when we have achieved our goal?

School and district self-assessments can be used not only when determining priorities for improvement initially, but also when monitoring progress in achieving improvement goals.

Engaging a critical friend can also be an effective way to monitor progress. Sometimes, it is helpful to have someone from outside the organization review progress on agreed upon indicators. A critical friend is someone you trust and who will provide open, honest, and direct feedback on predetermined criteria. A critical friend can look at a situation through fresh eyes and help school members gain insights that they might not see on their own.

Earlier in this chapter, we discussed the SEF as a tool used in Ontario for schools to conduct self-assessments. The SEF is used not only for school self-assessments but also for district reviews. The district reviews are conducted by system teams that consist of central office staff and school administrators. The intent of the district review is to provide schools with an impartial assessment of their school's effectiveness. The district review team acts as a critical friend. It conducts a school visit, examining predetermined indicators and providing feedback in a nonevaluative way. The process is about professional learning and continuous improvement; it is not an evaluation of the school principal or teachers. The intent is to inform the school improvement process. The information gathered in district reviews is helpful in two ways. First, it provides valuable observations to the school improvement team for their future planning. Second, by conducting reviews in many schools across the district, system leaders can determine trends and gather data that will help inform the district improvement process.

It is critical to the improvement process both at the district and school levels to develop a comprehensive monitoring system so that progress can be tracked and adjustments made to the plan to ensure continuous improvement. Improvement processes can only be deemed successful if they result in improved student learning.

Lessons Learned

As work within Ontario continues, it has become evident that the complex and varied strategies that have been implemented need to be explicitly interconnected and aligned. If key stakeholders do not see these strategies as integral components of a coherent improvement system, they may become overwhelmed and overlook their relevance, misconstruing them as disparate elements of a disintegrated whole. Alignment is critical to success.

Developing and implementing an improvement planning process can be a challenging task, and one that often requires several iterations and developmental changes as it becomes a part of the fabric of any system. Ontario's experience was no different, and there were several key lessons learned:

- Monitoring matters.
- Differentiation is a key.
- Plans must be focused on a few key, overarching areas with an alignment of strategies.
- Full system improvement requires focus on processes and people above content.

Monitoring Matters

As an educational system observes evidence that compels them to effect a change in practice after careful reflection and planning, the successful implementation of change strategies will hinge heavily on monitoring of practice and outcome. Monitoring involves not only determining whether improvement strategies are being implemented consistently, but also measuring progress in improved student achievement. In Ontario, we found that improvement was only possible when everyone charged with the implementation of improvement strategies was also intimately involved in monitoring progress. Building capacity with educators so that they were confident in assessing their own effectiveness was a key factor in Ontario's success in improving student achievement.

Differentiation Is Key

It is important to recognize that all districts and schools have unique characteristics. Improvement efforts will only succeed if we recognize those differences and allow a degree of flexibility in establishing improvement efforts. That being said, there are some recognized factors that, if in place, will assist in continuous improvement. To assist districts and schools, it is helpful to develop some common frameworks that will support improvement efforts while still allowing for local autonomy. In other words, we recognized that a one-size-fits-all approach would not work, but that there were some common actions that everyone needed to put into place. Dufour (2007) talks about the importance of "loose-tight" leadership. He states that such leadership fosters autonomy and creativity within a systematic framework that stipulates clear, nondiscretionary priorities and parameters.

In Ontario, we developed common frameworks for system improvement to provide a foundation for consistent action—the "prescribed adequacy" that Mourshed et al. (2010) described as a precursor to "unleashing greatness" through the work of educators within such a framework. Once these frameworks were established, a critical element of implementation surfaced: the need to allow for the molding of the frameworks to fit the individual circumstances and contexts of the districts or schools involved. This differentiation of application was necessary for several reasons. Different districts and schools within those districts had unique needs. Within the schools, different classrooms, departments, or divisions may have had varying strengths and needs on which an improvement focus was needed. A second reason was to allow for a molding of the process by the staff charged with carrying out the improvement strategies. The engagement of staff in the process of conducting the needs assessment and deriving the key goals and strategies is essential to their understanding and subsequent engagement in the task of effecting changes in practice. Although a system-wide goal is required, it needs to allow for some flexibility for individual schools, so that while a goal may be the improvement in a particular element of literacy as reflected in the system's provincial test results, each school needs to reflect on what its contribution will be and whether it will be able to focus on that element in addition to others, especially if it is already doing well in addressing that learning need. Again, the system would need to develop assessments of the learning needs that would allow that school to monitor its progress in changing student learning results without having to wait for provincial testing scores after the year has ended.

Focus and Alignment

With improvement cycles, research (e.g., Reeves, 2009; Schmoker, 2011) indicates that only a small number of priorities should be addressed in an improvement plan. Attempting to address a large number results in an ineffective disbursement of resources and attention, resulting in educators feeling frustrated and overwhelmed. Keeping improvement focused to a few critical goals and allowing for individual flexibility within smaller elements of the system are two keys to success. Related to this is the capacity at all levels of the education system to understand how various supports for education are related and aligned. Where connections can be observed and made explicit, resources can be pooled, and initiatives and strategies can be presented clearly to staff as an array of tools with which to address learning needs.

Pay Attention to Processes and People

As systems work to address learning needs and teaching practice in a broad fashion for all students in the system, the focus needs to move from the *what* of education (the curriculum standards and content) to the *how* of education (the processes of implementing curriculum, good pedagogy, assessment and evaluation practice, how we listen to students etc.). In Ontario, this meant engaging district leaders, school administrators, teachers, school support staff, teachers unions, politicians, community members, and parents in the discussion of processes being used to achieve improvement goals. Gathering feedback along the way was critical to the Ontario strategy. Processes were modified as data were gathered to further refine the strategy. Current research played a pivotal role in determining the processes that would be used. These processes were then tailored to meet local needs. One of the most powerful messages that was reinforced throughout our improvement process is that people matter most in any reform effort. The perspective of those who do the work must be incorporated throughout the process. This contributes to energy, motivation, and the desire and will to stay the course.

Summary

To improve graduation rates, districts and schools must see a need for improve. They need to examine the current state and envision their preferred future. Improvement will only happen if everyone who has responsibility for our students is engaged in the process and has ownership of the outcomes. Only then will we begin to see results. We cannot be satisfied with the status quo; too many of our students are not reaching the goal of graduation. By working together, districts and schools can develop an effective blueprint for improvement. Improvement planning is a cyclical and continuous process. Our efforts must be never ending. The process is one of analysis of data, determining the greatest area of need, building capacity, implementing required strategies, monitoring progress, and revising our efforts as needs evolve. The evidence is clear: When we get it right, the result is greater success for our students.

How to Re-Create These Strategies

Fundamental Beliefs: Effective district and school improvement processes can lead to success.

Key Strategies:

- Establish a district or school improvement team that is representative of the organization.

- Collaboratively develop a self-assessment based on research-informed indicators related to improved student learning.
- Determine the current status and the preferred future for students.
- Determine the greatest area of need for students and establish a small number of SMART goals.
- Establish ambitious yet attainable achievement targets.
- Ensure that the improvement plan is developed collaboratively.
- Establish a few research-informed strategies to achieve goals and implement those strategies deeply.
- Provide necessary resources and professional learning to support those responsible for implementation of the plan.
- Monitor progress regularly and communicate with all stakeholders.
- Engage critical friends to assist in monitoring progress and facilitate discussions about next steps.
- Revise the plan as needed.
- Celebrate successes.
- Evaluate the effectiveness of the plan and lessons learned to inform next steps.

Engaging All Staff: Teachers and school administrator engagement is critical in the implementation of any successful improvement initiative. Working together to examine student data can be eye-opening. When staff work together to analyze the current reality and discuss their hopes, dreams, and expectations for their students, they recognize the moral purpose of their work. Providing staff with an active role in the improvement process will build ownership. Inviting input regarding professional learning that will support improvement efforts will show staff that they will be supported. Sharing progress regularly is important; teacher efficacy improves when they see that their efforts make a difference.

Resources and Supports: The reality today is that many schools and districts have limited resources. That is why it is so important to determine priorities and align resources accordingly. Too often, we see funds spent simply because they were spent in that manner the previous year. The old saying "If you keep doing what you are doing, you will keep getting the same results" applies in this situation. To support new priorities, you will undoubtedly have to stop doing some things. When we are faced with "no new dollars," we have to be creative and focused in aligning our budget to the strategies that matter most at this particular point in time. Work with staff to collaboratively determine priorities for precious budget dollars.

Key Point: Effective improvement processes do not take more money; they take a willingness to look inward and make changes where needed.

References

Australia Capital Territory Department of Education and Training. (2009). *The school improvement framework.* Canberra, ACT: Author. Retrieved from http://www.det.act.gov.au/_data/assets/pdf_file/011/64298/School_Improvement_Framework.pdf

Benjamin, S. (2011, May). Simple leadership techniques: Rubrics, checklists, and structured collaboration. *Phi Delta Kappan, 92*(8), 25–31.

Dufour, R. (2007, November). In praise of top-down leadership: What drives your school improvement efforts—evidence of best practice or the pursuit of universal buy-in? *The School Administrator, 10*(64), 38–42.

Levin, B. (2008). *How to change 5000 schools: A practical and positive approach for leading change at every level.* Cambridge, MA: Harvard Education Press.

Lezotte, L. (2005). More effective schools: Professional learning communities in action. In R. Dufour, R. Eaker, & R. Dufour (Eds.), *On common ground: the power of professional learning communities* (pp. 177–191). Bloomington, IN: National Education Service.

Marzano, R. (2003). *What works in schools: Translating research into action.* Alexandria, VA: ASCD.

Mourshed, Mona, Chijioke, Chenezi, & Barber, Michael. (2010). *How the world's most improved school systems keep getting better.* New York: McKinsey & Company.

Ofsted. (2006, July 4). *Best practice in self-evaluation: A survey of schools, colleges and local authorities.* Manchester, UK: Author. Retrieved from http://www.ofsted.gov.uk/resources/best-practice-self-evaluation-survey-of-schools-colleges-and-local-authorities

Ontario Ministry of Education. (2010). *School effectiveness framework: A support for school improvement and student success.* Toronto: Queen's Printer for Ontario.

Ontario Ministry of Education, Literacy and Numeracy Secretariat. (2008). *The school effectiveness framework: A collegial process for continued growth in the effectiveness of Ontario elementary schools.* Toronto: Queen's Printer for Ontario.

Reeves, D. (2009). *Leading change in your school.* Alexandria, VA. ASCD.

Schmoker, M. J. (2005). Here and now: Improving teaching and learning. In R. Dufour, R. E. Eaker, & R. B. Dufour (Eds.), *On common ground: The power of professional learning communities* (pp. xi–xvi). Bloomington, IN: National Education Service.

Schmoker, M. J. (2011). *Focus: Elevating the essentials to radically improve student learning.* Alexandria, VA: ASCD.

4

High-Impact Strategies for Elementary Schools

If we are to be successful in achieving our goal to improve graduation rates, we must ensure that elementary schools lay the foundation for excellence and equity. For school districts to improve graduation rates, they must first examine the quality of their educational system from kindergarten right through to Grade 12. Research has clearly shown that academic success in elementary school is a strong predictor of success in high school. Hammond, Linton, Smink, and Drew (2007) found that low achievement was a major predictor linked to dropping out of high school. It is, therefore, essential that our schools help all students succeed academically from an early age.

As mentioned earlier, Ontario students in Grades 3, 6, and 9 are required to participate in annual provincial assessments. It is evident from data gathered over a number of years that students who do well on the provincial assessment in the primary (Grades 1–3) and junior (Grades 4–6) grades will most likely maintain their high level of achievement in secondary school. Ensuring that students are successful in the early years of their schooling will give them a greater chance of graduating. It is essential, therefore, that elementary schools provide the skills and knowledge that will enable students to achieve success in high school. In Ontario, as in many jurisdictions that have improved graduation rates, improvement efforts were directed at elementary schools as well as high schools.

Maintain a Clear Focus and Stay the Course

The priority in Ontario was to identify a small number of precise goals, along with a few key strategies to achieve those goals, and to build capacity at all levels to ensure deep implementation of the improvement initiatives. The government also ensured that the necessary resources were in place to support those responsible for implementation.

The focus in this chapter is to provide an overview of the key strategies that were used to improve academic results in elementary schools and close gaps in student achievement. While the strategies we discuss are specific to the Ontario context, it has been noted that other jurisdictions could benefit from examining the Ontario strategy and applying lessons learned to their own context.

In their report *How the World's Most Improved School Systems Keep Getting Better*, Mourshed, Chijioke, and Barber (2010) studied 20 systems from across the globe that had achieved substantial and sustained improvement in student achievement as measured by national and international assessments. In this report, they show that significant improvement in student achievement can be achieved in as little as six years. Ontario was one of the 20 systems highlighted in this report. The authors feel that their findings will help other systems replicate this success. In their study, they found that despite the fact that all school systems are unique, there were some common interventions that all of these improving systems adopted at some point along their improvement journey. Ontario is identified within this report as a "sustained improver," a system that has seen five or more years of consistent improvement, one that the authors refer to as a "great system." The strategies used in Ontario parallel many of the interventions used in other jurisdictions that have shown continuous improvement.

In Ontario, the elementary school improvement strategy was spearheaded by the Literacy and Numeracy Secretariat. This branch of the Ministry of Education was charged with improving student outcomes for students in the elementary grades. The foundation for improvement was based on improving literacy and numeracy skills for all elementary students, increasing the knowledge base of the profession, building alliances with all those who had a stake in public education, and striving for not just excellence but also equity in student outcomes.

The Secretariat was committed to forging consensus around the goals, strategies, resources, and tools that were needed to ensure excellence in teaching and learning. This was done in a number of ways. First of all, the Secretariat established a strong focus on literacy and numeracy, and this remained the focus for a number of years. Too often, educators are bombarded with new initiatives with little or no professional support for implementation. They are not afforded sufficient time to ensure deep implementation before another wave of new priorities engulfs them. In Ontario, educators were provided detailed information about the improvement strategy. Input was sought from a range of professional organizations such as teacher unions, principal organizations, and director and superintendent associations. Partnerships were also formed with school trustee groups, parent associations, and other community organizations. This was done through provincial and regional meetings and conferences, visits to local school boards, meetings with heads of organizations, and consultations with target groups. Great effort was put forth to engage all stakeholders in conversations about the need for improvement and what was required to make the necessary changes. To assist educators with the implementation of new strategies, professional learning opportunities were provided as well as professional and classroom resources. Regular memos and communiqués provided updates and progress reports. We acknowledged the good things that were happening in many districts and schools and built on the spirit of innovation that already existed in many schools and districts across the province. Connecting with not just the minds of educators but also their hearts was key in helping them see the urgency in improving student outcomes. Our experience has been that most, if not all, teachers enter the profession because they want to make a difference in the lives of the students. Principals also reflect the best of the profession in their commitment and tenacity.

The Secretariat also recognized the unique nature of every district and the importance of garnering support through empowering districts to develop local solutions to improve student learning. Shortly after its inception, the Secretariat provided resources and support for local district initiatives, based on needs identified locally by school districts. This strategy recognized that a combination of bottom-up identification of priorities and top-down supports would more effectively engage educators in the improvement efforts. Over 170 local projects were funded in the first year. The projects ranged from district-wide initiatives involving thousands of students, to smaller pilot projects that focused on a small number of schools. Districts were expected to monitor the impact of their projects and report back to the Secretariat on outcomes. This resulted in the compilation of provincially developed strategies that had a positive impact on student achievement.

When given the opportunity to be actively involved in the improvement process, to provide input, and to use their expertise to improve educational opportunities for students, most educators are highly motivated to take an active role in the change process. The Ontario strategy built goodwill, affirmed the professionalism of teachers, and enhanced the motivation of all who worked in education to improve our schools. Through this collaborative approach, the Secretariat created a shared sense of purpose and instilled a sense of urgency to make Ontario's education system the best it could be for the benefit of the students.

The approach taken for this massive reform effort involved engagement at all levels. It was necessary to align efforts at the provincial, district, school, and classroom levels. At the provincial level, policies were established and resources allocated that provided much-needed support to schools and districts. For example, the provincial government provided additional funds for textbooks and libraries, new resources for professional learning, and all-day early learning kindergarten programs. It also reduced primary class sizes. The Secretariat sought input from school board administrators, teachers' unions, trustees, parent groups, and other stakeholders as the provincial strategy was developed. School boards were expected to establish local improvement teams and develop, implement, and monitor improvement plans with the assistance of ministry of education staff.

The Secretariat developed a nine-point strategy to guide its actions.

Strategy 1

Help school districts set ambitious achievement targets that reflect high expectations for student learning and assist in developing improvement plans to operationalize the targets.

Strategy 2

Establish and support teams of educators at the regional, board, and school levels to drive continuous improvement in literacy and numeracy.

Strategy 3

Help classroom teachers focus on success for all students and take advantage of smaller class sizes in the primary grades by providing training on effective teaching practices and the use of assessment data to guide instruction.

Strategy 4

Provide resources and professional learning to build the capacity of district and school leaders to implement effective practices in literacy and numeracy instruction.

Strategy 5

Allocate resources to support target setting and school and district planning to support continuous improvement, while taking into account local conditions and avoiding one-size-fits-all solutions.

Strategy 6

Mobilize the system to provide equity in student outcome both by raising awareness and by providing professional development to target interventions for selected groups that continue to underperform, such as Aboriginal students, English-language learners, students in special education programs, and boys.

Strategy 7

Embark on a process of community outreach and engagement, including student leaders, trustees, and parents, to build support for the literacy and numeracy initiative.

Strategy 8

Demonstrate a commitment to research- and evidence-based inquiry and decision making, and find effective ways to share this information with school districts and the public system at large.

Strategy 9

Establish Ontario's presence on the national and international scene as a jurisdiction that is both learning from and contributing to the knowledge base about how to improve literacy and numeracy achievement.

As well as raising the bar overall, the government committed to closing the gaps in achievement, with targeted strategies to support equity of outcomes. Provincial data indicated that certain student groups continued to struggle to achieve at higher levels and that gaps in performance continued to be large. For example, students whose first language was not English or French, students with special educational needs, and boys' literacy acquisition continued to be areas of concern. Provincial assessment data, local district and school data, and other evidence also indicated the need to continue to focus action to support Aboriginal students, students from other minority ethnic groups, and students living in poverty.

The preceding nine strategies were informed by evidence about the current status of student achievement in Ontario and through the analysis of needs identified through the experience of working directly in and with districts and schools, as well as lessons from international reform efforts, including research on how to effectively build and sustain improvement. A key driving theme became the emphasis on capacity building at all levels of the system. A priority for the Secretariat was to provide a range of professional learning opportunities that would increase the capacity of educators to implement improvement strategies. We facilitated the development of teams of professionals that would work together for improvement and fostered partnerships, working collaboratively within and across provincial, district, and school levels. The emphasis on partnerships and collaboration was particularly important in a context where previous relations between government, districts, and schools in Ontario had become strained during the former government, due to a range of factors including labor disruptions and a perceived lack of respect for the teaching profession. The strategies were also informed by an understanding that partnerships with parents and community members are important in supporting both student achievement and wider confidence in public education.

The Secretariat recognized that a completely top-down or one-size-fits-all approach would not work. Supports were provided that recognized the diverse needs of district school boards and schools across the province. The focus was to provide the necessary supports for improvement to all boards, but the Secretariat also provided more intense support to those districts and schools that were struggling the most. The result was improved student achievement and increased capacity for administrators and staff to plan effectively for improvement and to change practice, when necessary.

A number of actions were taken to implement the Secretariat's nine key strategies, including the following:

- Hiring a highly skilled and dedicated team of instructional leaders and curriculum specialists as student achievement officers to provide direct support to schools and school districts

- Working with boards and schools to develop, implement, and monitor improvement plans with precise goals and clearly defined strategies to achieve targets
- Supporting the effective use of data to inform decision making, track student progress, and intervene early when students were struggling to succeed
- Embedding a strong research orientation to find, understand, and share effective practices
- Providing a range of vehicles for capacity building (e.g., direct training for teachers and principals; the production of teacher resources, webcasts, and monographs outlining high-impact strategies)
- Providing targeted interventions to the lowest-achieving schools and those that have been static in their improvement through the Ontario Focused Intervention Partnership (OFIP) strategy
- Facilitating improvement efforts by providing district boards with financial support to initiate local improvement projects that met their unique needs
- Creating a network of schools, known as Schools on the Move, that had demonstrated continuous improvement to facilitate lateral capacity building and to share successful practices
- Implementing character education programs based on community engagement and locally identified character attributes (e.g., respect, responsibility, honesty, fairness, empathy, courage, optimism)
- Funding tutoring programs to ensure that struggling students received additional support
- Developing a School Effectiveness Framework that outlined key components of effective schools, identified indicators of success, and encouraged the notion of professional accountability
- Creating a data-analysis tool, known as Statistical Neighbours, to assist boards and schools in using data to improve student achievement by removing the excuses for low performance
- Developing a network of district school boards that included some of the lowest- and highest-achieving boards in the province to identify challenges, share successful practices, and build capacity

The result of the reform strategy has been a steady increase in student achievement as measured by the elementary school provincial assessments.

Not only has there been continuous improvement, but there has also been a reduction in achievement gaps. From 2002–2003 to 2010–2011,

Figure 4.1   Overall Achievement Growth

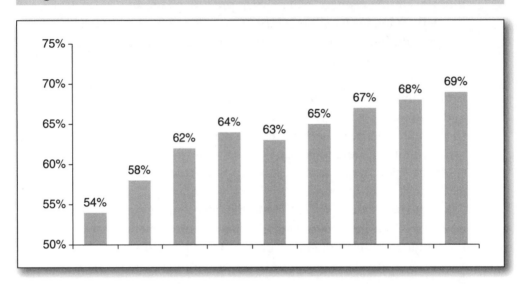

students in special education programs and English-language learners showed marked improvement in reading and writing as measured by provincial assessments administered by EQAO. Figure 4.1 shows the achievement gains for all students in Ontario, while Table 4.1 shows gains for selected groups. A one percentage gain equals 1500 students.

Table 4.1   Results for Selected Groups

English Language Learners

- ✓ Improved 29 percentage points in primary reading
- ✓ Improved 32 percentage points in primary writing
- ✓ Improved 32 percentage points in junior reading
- ✓ Improved 37 percentage points in junior writing

Students in Special Education Programs

- ✓ Improved 14 percentage points in primary reading
- ✓ Improved 34 percentage points in primary writing
- ✓ Improved 20 percentage points in junior reading
- ✓ Improved 24 percentage points in junior writing

Target Setting: The Power of High Expectations

Critical to the success of any school system is coupling high expectations with appropriate supports for students. One of the greatest barriers to improving student achievement is the belief that some students cannot achieve at high levels. Yet, experience has clearly shown us that even schools in challenging circumstances can achieve at high levels. One way to communicate high expectations is to establish ambitious targets for achievement, and that is exactly what Ontario did.

Targets provide a commitment to mobilizing the system and working toward a preferred future. When districts and schools establish achievement targets, they are communicating clearly the improvement that they are striving to achieve by a particular point in time. Targets provide a focus for efforts and act as mile markers on the road to improvement. Once targets are established, district and school teams can start the conversation about the steps needed to achieve those targets. They can prioritize resources when their efforts are more focused.

Early on in their mandate, the provincial government established targets for literacy and numeracy in elementary school as well as a high school graduation target. The first step in realizing excellence was to require that every elementary student develop effective skills in reading, writing, and mathematics by Grade 6 (about age 12). They established a provincial target, namely, that 75 % of Ontario students should, with the right supports, achieve at least a Level 3 (equivalent to a B or 70%) on provincial assessments in these areas.

Having established the expectation of targets at the provincial level, the Ministry required all school districts and schools to establish ambitious achievement targets as well. The approach taken in Ontario was that districts would identify their own targets for improvement toward the overall provincial goal for student achievement. The specific strategy for generating targets varied with local districts, some starting with school targets and then establishing the overall district strategy, and others setting their overall target first and then working to identify individual school targets. Once targets were established, boards and schools developed improvement plans that outlined strategies to achieve targets, timelines, and means for measuring progress.

During this process, we learned that setting targets that were appropriate required professional dialogue and development to balance ambitious and realistic goals for improvement. In the first round of target setting, some districts set very low or even negative targets, fearing that they might be embarrassed publicly if they were not able to achieve their goal. Student achievement officers from the Secretariat worked directly with school district leaders to assist them in establishing realistic targets that were embedded in district and school improvement plans with actions linked to achievement goals. This process included professional learning opportunities focused on the use of data to inform decisions at district and school levels, plus the provision of a resource document that provided research information about effective improvement planning processes (Ontario Ministry of Education, 2006).

At the same time that educators were setting ambitious targets for student achievement, they were also receiving a variety of supports to strengthen their professional practice. Positive pressure and targeted support was a keystone to success in Ontario. Administrators and teachers were provided with ongoing professional learning opportunities, resources were developed to support classroom instruction, class sizes were reduced to provide more individualized instruction, and ministry staff supported school improvement efforts. The Ontario strategy recognized that to improve our schools, we must invest in, support, and develop people and validate their efforts.

The Importance of Building Capacity

Research has shown that the quality of classroom instruction and school leadership has a direct impact on student achievement. Therefore, for school systems to improve student outcomes, they must ensure that educators have not only the will but also the skill to improve instruction. They need to invest in their people and build capacity to ensure that all students receive a high-quality education. Barber and Mourshed (2009) stress the importance of the quality of classroom instruction and school leadership. They point out that "over three years, learning with a high-performing teacher instead of a low-performing teacher can make a 53 percentile difference for two students who start at the same achievement level" (p. 27). They state that there is no more important empirical determinant of student outcomes than good teaching. They also point out that second only to the quality of teaching is school leadership. They state that replacing an "average principal" with an outstanding principal in an "average school" could increase student achievement by over 20 percentile points. Based on current research about the importance of capacity building, the underlying foundation for reform in Ontario rested with a commitment to build capacity among educators at all levels to improve teaching and learning. Making capacity building a priority provides educators with the knowledge and skill to effectively implement improvement strategies. As Fullan (2005) points out, "There is no chance that large-scale reform will happen, let alone stick, unless capacity building is a central component of the strategy for improvement" (p. 11).

The Secretariat provided a wide range of supports for district leaders, school administrators, and teachers. To strengthen literacy and numeracy skills, teachers were provided with extensive and carefully targeted professional development. Both provincial and regional conferences were held that provided practical strategies to support teachers in differentiating instruction. Teachers were also provided training related to high-impact strategies for teaching reading and other instructional strategies. The Secretariat collaborated with the teachers' unions to provide summer institutes on a variety of topics. Tens of thousands of teachers attended these sessions on a voluntary basis.

Recognizing that teachers had varied professional learning needs, the Secretariat produced a wide range of webcasts that provided "anywhere, anytime" professional learning opportunities. The webcasts featured global experts in the field of education who shared current research on effective instructional strategies. In addition, Ontario educators shared promising practices and lessons learned. The webcasts covered topics such as boys and literacy, high-impact strategies for teaching mathematics, differentiating instruction, board improvement planning, equity of outcomes, reading instruction, leadership development, and character development, to name a few. Educators across the province provided suggestions for topics that they felt would be valuable to their practice. The response from educators regarding this form of professional learning was overwhelmingly positive. It provided yet one more avenue for educators to strengthen their knowledge and skills and to develop a strong research orientation. These webcasts can be found at www.curriculum.org/content/webcasts.

The Secretariat developed a publication titled "The Capacity Building Series." This series provided teachers with professional advice on a range of topics that included, but were not limited to, teacher moderation, learning blocks for literacy and numeracy, professional learning communities, student self-assessment, nonfiction writing, character education, and collaborative teacher inquiry. Teachers were also provided with a wide range of guidebooks and professional manuals. Resources developed by the Secretariat can be found online at www.edu.gov.on .ca/eng/literacynumeracy/ publications.html.

Capacity Building in Ontario's Elementary Schools

Ontario provided a wide range of professional learning opportunities for educators, recognizing the varied learning needs throughout the profession:

- ✓ Direct training for teachers and principals
- ✓ Leadership development
- ✓ Webcasts by leading international experts
- ✓ Research monographs
- ✓ Print resources
- ✓ Sharing successful practices (Schools on the Move)
- ✓ Networking opportunities for district leaders
- ✓ Development of professional learning communities and networks
- ✓ Coaching
- ✓ Summer institutes for teachers

Educators were given opportunities for job-embedded professional learning. The Secretariat employed a large number of highly skilled educators from across the province as SAOs. The SAOs had a proven record as curriculum and instructional leaders. Their role was to work in partnership with district leaders, principals, and teachers to develop improvement plans, build capacity at all levels of the school system, and implement high-impact strategies to improve student achievement. Their daily work was in the field rather than in government offices. They focused on creating a positive and demanding work culture that stressed high expectations within the context of a strong learning culture characterized by innovation, creativity, and a strong results orientation. The SAOs acted as critical friends; they provided advice, asked the tough questions, and coached and supported educators in the field in their improvement efforts. Their role was to support and coach, not to evaluate or make judgements.

Schools were encouraged to establish professional learning communities where teachers and principals could learn together. The Secretariat provided networking opportunities for teachers and district and school administrators so they could share their successes, identify challenges, and work together to find solutions. Some of the best systems in the world find ways to enable teachers to work and learn together (Barber & Mourshed, 2007).

Another powerful learning opportunity was the Schools on the Move initiative, where educators were provided the opportunity to learn firsthand from schools that had demonstrated continuous improvement. To highlight and share successful practices, the Secretariat initiated the program in 2006. Each year, the Secretariat identified schools that had made substantial progress in raising student achievement and sustaining that progress. These schools are a model for demonstrating that high levels of achievement are possible, even in the most economically challenged communities. The central theme of the program is "schools learning from other schools." Schools that have been selected as "schools on the move" reflect the rich diversity of Ontario. These schools are from all parts of the province—public and Catholic, French and English—and are located in all types of communities.

> Schools on the Move are exciting places for children and teachers, not just because everyone is learning but also because staff members understand and can describe the practices and strategies that make a difference to their learning as well as to their students' learning. (Ontario Ministry of Education, Literacy and Numeracy Secretariat, 2007, p. 6)

To be selected as a school on the move, schools must demonstrate continuous improvement in EQAO scores and be able to articulate the strategies used to improve student achievement. They must be able to provide classroom evidence of progress being made in student achievement and demonstrate the implementation of the research-informed strategies that have proven successful in improving student achievement. The Secretariat conducted school visits to gather further information to be used in the selection process. These schools act as a resource for other schools in the province so that the latter can learn from the successes of the former and replicate promising strategies in their own schools.

Each year, the Secretariat distributed a "Schools on the Move" publication, which presented profiles of each newly recognized school and contact information. This was highly valuable to schools across the province that wanted to connect with these schools to learn with and from them. A provincial forum was held annually to celebrate the achievements of these schools, highlight successful strategies, and provide an opportunity for networking. Staff from selected schools shared their experiences in a variety of ways. They presented at conferences, welcomed visitors to their schools, communicated online with colleagues across the province, and visited other schools.

A Strong Commitment to Research

A strong commitment to research, evidence-based inquiry, and data-informed decision making were critical to the success of the elementary school strategy. Early in the Secretariat's mandate, research was conducted within the province of Ontario to determine the strategies used in district school boards that were achieving continuous improvement. In the report *Unlocking Potential for Learning*, Campbell, Fullan, and Glaze (2006) share strategies that these districts had in common that positively impacted student achievement. They identified 12 key components of effective practices that linked to four broad strategic areas:

1. Leading With Purpose and Focusing Direction
   - Leadership for learning was a priority. Leadership was purposeful and focused on supporting learning.
   - The districts had a shared vision and focused on student achievement as the priority.
   - The districts believed in their moral responsibility to educate all students to the highest possible level. They believed that all students could learn with sufficient supports and time.

2. Designing a Coherent Strategy, Coordinating Implementation, and Reviewing Outcomes

- The districts had a planned, coherent, and coordinated overarching strategy for improvement.
- Resources were prioritized to focus on improved student achievement.
- The districts developed an effective organization to support their focus on student achievement. In some cases, this meant reorganizing district roles and responsibilities to ensure supports and personnel were aligned to district improvement priorities.
- The districts ensured system- and school-level monitoring, review, feedback, and accountability were in place.

3. Developing Precision in Knowledge, Skills, and Daily Practices for Improving Learning

- Capacity building and professional learning for teachers and principals was a top priority.
- Curriculum development, instruction, and interventions to improve teaching and learning for all students were supported.
- The districts were committed to using data for informing system-wide planning and decision making.

4. Sharing Responsibility Through Building Partnerships

- The districts fostered positive and purposeful partnerships.
- Two-way communication and a sense of common direction were established. The districts all emphasized a clear and consistent message about raising student achievement.

This research was shared with districts across the province. Districts began to network with "like districts" to share successful practice and to learn from one another.

One of the first research projects conducted by the Secretariat was known as the "Sites of Excellence" project. The purpose was to identify classrooms where practical and effective classroom strategies were contributing to student success and improved achievement in literacy and numeracy. School districts across the province were asked to identify one or more schools or one or more classrooms that they considered to exhibit successful practices. Schools were identified where leadership and capacity-building activities were effectively supporting improved student performance in literacy and numeracy. A total of

163 sites (school and classroom) provided information about their identified practices to the Secretariat. We found that many of these schools used many of the same successful practices. These included

- staff collaboration,
- establishment of effective professional learning communities,
- job-embedded professional learning,
- classroom practice that was aligned to the school improvement plan,
- engagement of parents in meaningful ways,
- the use of data to inform instruction,
- flexible instructional groupings within classrooms,
- uninterrupted blocks of time for literacy and numeracy,
- a balanced literacy program, and
- integrating literacy and numeracy across the curriculum.

Providing access to current research on effective practice was a priority for the Secretariat. In partnership with Ontario universities' faculties of education, the Secretariat launched an innovative series of monographs titled "What Works: Research Into Practice." This series highlights promising practices that are research informed and are written by scholars from Ontario universities who are experts in their field. These monographs are being used by educators across the globe as they are able to access them free of charge.

Research was conducted in a variety of areas to determine effective practices when working with Ontario's diverse population. Using research-informed, high-impact instructional strategies has resulted in improved student achievement at all levels. In addition, ongoing research has determined provincial trends, strengths, and areas in need of improvement. To further strengthen links to research, policy, and practice, the Ontario Ministry of Education hosts the annual Ontario Education Research Symposium.

Make Early Learning a Top Priority

Research has clearly shown that providing high-quality early learning experiences for students has a positive impact on future learning. Unfortunately, many children do not have access to high-quality early learning opportunities. In some jurisdictions, only those children whose parents have the financial means to send them to nursery schools and early learning centers benefit from such experiences. In an equitable society, all children should have equal access to high-quality early learning.

In Ontario, it is compulsory for all students age six and older to attend school. In addition, for decades, Ontario has offered senior and junior kindergarten programs for the province's four- and five-year-old students. These programs were generally offered for half days or alternate days and provided a bridge between early child development and the more formal full-day compulsory program.

A series of early years reports (McCain & Mustard, 1999; McCain, Mustard, & McCuaig, 2011; McCain, Mustard, & Shanker, 2007) provided the background that would inform the Ontario early years strategy. The first report stressed the critical nature of early learning; the authors pointed out that "It is clear that the early years from conception to age six have the most important influence of any time in the life cycle on brain development and subsequent learning, behaviour and health" (McCain & Mustard, 1999, p. 6). The benefits of quality early childhood development programs are many, ranging from better academic performance to improved health, reduced poverty, and general societal well-being. This is stressed in the second early years report:

> Well funded, integrated, child development and parenting programs improve the cognitive and social functioning of all children. If properly linked to labour, health, and social services, early childhood programs can deliver additional outcomes, such as enhanced maternal employment, less family poverty. . . . Quality early childhood programs are not only good for children and families, they are good for the bottom line. (McCain et al., 2007, p. 135)

Recognizing the importance of early learning, Ontario introduced full-day kindergarten for four- and five-year-olds beginning in 2010. The program is being phased in, with full implementation expected by 2014. The government stipulated the size of the classes and the program that would be implemented. As full-day, everyday kindergarten was introduced, a revised curriculum, "The Full-Day Early Learning–Kindergarten Program," was also implemented. The goals of the program are to

- "establish a strong foundation for the early years by providing young children with an integrated day of learning;
- provide a play-based learning environment;
- help children to make a smoother transition to Grade 1;
- improve children's progress for success in school and their lives beyond school" (Ontario Ministry of Education, 2011, p. 20)

Each classroom has an early learning–Kindergarten team that consists of a kindergarten teacher and an early childhood educator (ECE) for every 26 students, making the adult to child ratio 1:13. The kindergarten teacher and ECE work in partnership to deliver the program that recognizes the unique needs of each student. The program is based on purposeful play that develops a sound foundation to support future academic success. The team provides whole-class, small-group, and individual instruction; independent and child-initiated learning opportunities; and activities at learning centers. The Early Learning–Kindergarten team gives the students many opportunities to investigate and explore. The team uses ongoing assessment to determine a student's strengths, needs, and interests, and then uses that information as a basis for program planning. The educators build on what the children know and help them to extend their thinking. Since oral language is the foundation for literacy, the Full-Day Early Learning–Kindergarten Program provides rich, language-focused activities. They provide literacy and numeracy instruction that is developmentally appropriate for the children. Student learning expectations for personal, social, and academic development are outlined in Ministry documents and guide the Early Learning–Kindergarten team's program planning. The importance of encouraging family involvement is also stressed in the kindergarten program.

The government has also provided guidelines and support to encourage districts and schools to enter into third-party agreements to offer before- or after-school programs, or both, for kindergarten students. This ensures seamless day care for parents so that they do not have to worry about transporting their children to other locations for before- and after-school care. Resources have been developed for before- and after-school care providers so that their program aligns with the kindergarten core program, ensuring that children have a consistent experience throughout their day.

Introducing full-day early learning kindergarten has required a major financial commitment from the Ontario government. This could potentially create barriers to implementation in some districts. In Ontario, the government decided that with the research being clear about the benefits of early childhood development, it was prepared to make full-day early learning kindergarten a budget priority. To plan effectively for the cost of the program, the government committed to a five-year phase in of the program. In collaboration with local school districts, schools were identified that would benefit most from early implementation, with other schools to be added over time. Reassessing priorities and resources and working with community partners are essential if districts are to commit to enhancing early childhood learning opportunities.

Focus on Literacy

Early school achievement, especially in reading and writing, is one of the greatest predictors of future success. Helping students attain strong literacy skills will facilitate success in all subject areas. Ontario recognized that the first step in improving student achievement for all students was to ensure that they have a sound literacy foundation. In the OECD report *No More Failures,* Field, Kuczera, and Pont (2007) point out that literacy provides an essential tool for working and living; it is a foundation for nearly all higher-order thinking skills. Research has shown that students who drop out of school often struggle with reading (Carbo, 2008). Schmoker (2011) also stresses the importance of a sound foundation in literacy; he writes, "Literacy is still the unrivalled, but grossly under-implemented, key to learning both content *and* thinking skills" (p. 11). It is essential, therefore, that all schools provide a solid foundation in literacy for all students.

In Ontario, we provided the necessary supports to ensure that schools established a sound foundation in literacy and taught literacy across all content areas. Reading instruction did not require students simply to read and recall facts, but also to use higher-order thinking skills, problem solving, and critical thinking. A key to success was providing opportunities for students to read by drawing inferences, supporting their opinions and arguments, drawing conclusions, comparing and contrasting, relating to their own experiences, critically analyzing the author's position, and relating to real-world issues and circumstances. Professional learning opportunities stressed the importance of uninterrupted blocks of time for literacy that would provide a comprehensive literacy program that included regular read-alouds, shared reading, modeled writing, guided reading and writing, and independent reading and writing. Summer institutes, provincial learning conferences, regional professional learning forums, and district and school capacity building focused on literacy instruction. The Ministry of Education provided additional funding to all districts to purchase resources for school libraries. These materials were to include both fiction and nonfiction, appropriate to a range of abilities and interests, and were to reflect the cultural diversity of their communities. SAOs also made literacy instruction the foundation of their work when visiting schools.

Current research regarding high-impact strategies was shared with schools. The importance of nonfiction writing was stressed. Reeves (2002) states that nonfiction writing is associated with higher test scores in reading, mathematics, science, and social studies. Recognizing that, much like other jurisdictions around the world, girls in Ontario were outperforming boys in literacy achievement, the literacy achievement gap between boys and girls had to be addressed. To support the development of strategies that would improve boys' literacy achievement, schools were given opportunities to enter into the Boys Literacy Teacher Inquiry Project. Through this project, schools were provided funds to develop innovative teaching strategies and purchase literary resources that appealed to boys. Teachers were provided enhanced professional learning and networking opportunities to share promising practices. Research results were shared across the province so that high-impact strategies could be replicated, and resources were developed to help develop teacher capacity.

Targeted Supports

Within Ontario, it was recognized that there were certain groups of students and certain schools that had demonstrated low achievement over an extended period. Provincial data was disaggregated to determine the groups of students who were disproportionately represented at the bottom of academic results. School data were examined as well to identify those schools that were the lowest achieving in the province so that targeted support could be provided to raise achievement levels. In many cases, these schools were facing challenging circumstances. Ontario realized that fairness didn't mean sameness. To help all students achieve, it is important for jurisdictions to differentiate their approaches to provide the supports necessary to improve achievement.

Ontario provided targeted supports in a variety of ways. Funding was given to school districts to implement tutoring programs for struggling students. Districts determined the schools with the greatest needs and then provided both in-school and after-school tutoring for students who were struggling with literacy and numeracy. Research has shown that structured tutoring programs conducted by well-trained volunteers can strengthen student literacy skills (Berrill, 2009). There is strong evidence that tutoring is an effective strategy for addressing the needs of low-performing students (Snow, 2003). For some children, especially those living in poverty, there is a drop in learning over the summer. These children, for the most part, lack the opportunity to take part in enriching activities such as summer camps or private lessons. Some of these children forget the foundational skills they have learned over the school year. To help avoid loss of learning over the summer, Ontario distributed funds for districts to provide summer learning programs for elementary school-age children. In addition, the province established a program known as the Ontario Focused Intervention Partnership to support its lowest-performing schools.

The Ontario Focused Intervention Partnership

Ontario schools that historically underperformed were provided with targeted support through an initiative that was known as the Ontario Focused Intervention Partnership (OFIP). Schools that took part in this initiative were some of the lowest-performing elementary schools in the province. The Ministry of Education, through the Secretariat, worked collaboratively with school districts to improve student achievement in these schools. Key to this initiative was professional learning and school-based capacity building to help schools implement high-impact instructional strategies that research has shown would improve student achievement.

The goals of OFIP were to

- achieve equity of outcomes for all students,
- provide intensive support for low-performing schools and "static" or "declining" schools,
- strengthen and support instructional leadership and classroom practices,
- implement research-informed strategies to improve student learning,
- share promising practices, and
- work collaboratively to build capacity in boards and schools to ensure long-term sustainability and high levels of student achievement.

Schools were identified to take part in OFIP based on their scores on the provincial assessments in Grades 3 and 6. Schools with less than 34% of their students at the provincial standard in reading for two of three consecutive years became OFIP schools, as well as those that had been static or declining over a three-year period. OFIP provided a range of supports for all boards in the province, but the most intensive support was provided for the lowest-performing schools. A key aspect of the strategy was for the Secretariat, through its SAOs, to build partnerships with school staff. This was not a punitive strategy; it was about providing not just positive pressure to improve but, more importantly, the necessary supports to make improvement possible. It was truly an initiative based on partnerships and collaborative support.

SAOs worked closely with school principals and their staff to develop a school improvement plan that would address the needs of the school. They assisted the staff in disaggregating their school achievement data to identify school strengths and determine the greatest area of need for their students. This was then formulated into a small number of key improvement goals and ambitious targets for improved student achievement. SAOs provided support in establishing an effective professional learning community that reflected on current practice, examined student achievement results, collaboratively assessed student work, and determined next steps and changes in practice that should be made. Together, they monitored progress and the effectiveness of the improvement plan on a regular basis. The SAOs met with the school principal and staff throughout the year to monitor progress, take part in staff meetings, discuss challenges, provide guidance on the implementation of strategies, and collaborate on ways to overcome barriers to improvement. The focus was to make school improvement a whole-school responsibility. These schools received support over a three-year period.

Being identified as an OFIP school was not easy for staff in those schools in the beginning. They were well aware that they were at the bottom of the provincial achievement results. Staff in these schools were hard working and deeply cared about their students, yet they were not getting the results they wanted. In many cases, they were frustrated and did not know what more they could do. The SAOs brought fresh eyes to the situation; serving as critical friends to these schools. By working collaboratively with the staff, they were able to identify schools' strengths and worked to build on those strengths. They also helped them to identify areas that needed improvement. By disaggregating school data, they identified a few key priorities for the school improvement plan. It was vital to not select too many goals and overwhelm staff. They focused on a small number of goals for implementation and then identified research-informed strategies collaboratively to help them achieve their goal. Regular monitoring of progress was essential to make revisions to the plan as necessary.

In our work across the province we found that there was great variation in the instructional practice and leadership between schools. Hopkins (2005), in his work in the United Kingdom, goes further to say that in his experience, "the range of variation within any school dwarfs the difference between schools in the UK by a factor of three to four times" (p. 4). We know that there are certain strategies that have been shown to improve student achievement, and yet the question we must ask is, if we know that they work, why are they not being used in every classroom and every school? Consistency in the implementation of high-impact instructional strategies is essential. We found that in many of our low-performing schools, there were some key elements that were missing. It was for that reason that we established some "nonnegotiables" for schools that were to be involved in OFIP.

To take part in the OFIP, schools were expected to put into place the following strategies to drive change:

- Establish uninterrupted blocks of time for literacy and numeracy.
- Implement a comprehensive literacy program.
- Use common assessment strategies that include diagnostic tools.
- Create a school improvement team.
- Conduct a school self-assessment to examine data, determine the school's strengths and weaknesses, establish improvement goals, identify instructional interventions, establish a mechanism for monitoring progress, and plan for next steps.
- Set ambitious achievement targets.
- Acquire resources to implement a comprehensive literacy and numeracy program.
- Develop a process to regularly monitor the growth and progress of specific students to ensure equity of outcomes.
- Provide early and ongoing interventions for struggling students.
- Implement strategies for communicating and celebrating progress.

Despite the fact that the OFIP schools had higher proportions of students living in poverty, higher proportions of English-language learners, and higher proportions of students with special education needs, the majority of these schools improved in a very short time. In the first year, 76% of the OFIP schools receiving the most intense support improved in Grade 3 reading as measured by the provincial assessment administered by EQAO; 66% of these schools improved in Grade 6 reading. They also saw improvements in writing and mathematics.

The key to success in the OFIP strategy was the consistent implementation of a few key strategies and time for staff to work together with a specific focus. For most of these schools, the focus began with literacy. That does not mean ignoring everything else, but it was felt that if student literacy improved, there would be a positive impact on all subject areas. In working with these schools, we learned a number of valuable lessons. We learned that targeted support and focused interventions work. We also learned that investing in people and building their capacity in the specific areas related to the school's improvement priorities were paramount to success. We found that when staff work collaboratively on the school improvement plan and the monitoring of its effectiveness, they develop ownership in improvement efforts. When improvement efforts have a narrow and precise focus, staff respond more positively, as they do not feel overwhelmed. When working with OFIP schools, staff told us that one of the things they appreciated most was the opportunity to come together to co-plan, reflect on practice, and learn together through job-embedded professional learning. Too often, teachers work in isolation and don't benefit from the combined expertise and knowledge of their colleagues.

We found that in many of the low-performing schools, staff had not established high expectations for their students. Setting high expectations for all students is critical to success. Setting ambitious school-wide achievement targets raises expectations and helps schools realize their goals. Schools need to reinforce continuously the message that all students can achieve and all teachers can teach to a high level. Focusing on excellence, however, is not enough; schools must also strive for equity of outcomes. Providing early and ongoing interventions for students who are struggling is critical to achieving equity.

School leadership is pivotal in guiding the improvement efforts of the school. In their research on leadership effects on student learning, Leithwood, Seashore Louis, Anderson, and Wahlstrom (2004) point out that "there are virtually no documented instances of troubled schools being turned around without the interventions by a powerful leader" (p. 5). They acknowledge that there are many other factors that contribute to improvement, but "leadership is the catalyst." The school principal has a key role to play in developing a learning culture where teachers reflect on their practice and work together to achieve improvement goals. The school administration needs to find creative ways to enable staff to meet together and to provide them with the resources they need. Budget decisions must support the goals in the school improvement plan if improvement efforts are to succeed. Principals should also do everything in their power to maintain a stable teaching team. We often found that in the lowest-performing schools, there were relatively high rates of principal and staff turnover. High staff turnover slows progress. School administrators should also ensure that success is celebrated regularly. Celebrating small successes keeps everyone motivated and they strive to move forward.

We found that in the OFIP schools that were highly successful in raising student achievement, principals made regular visits to classrooms to monitor progress and support staff in the implementation of school priorities. Teachers provided their students with higher-order thinking skills in all subject areas. Literacy instruction was provided across the curriculum. Teachers differentiated instruction to meet the wide range of learning needs in their classroom. Students were given multiple opportunities to revise their work based on precise and timely feedback from their teachers. A variety of assessment techniques were used, and students engaged in self-assessment with the use of exemplars, rubrics, and anchor charts. Every classroom had uninterrupted blocks of time for the effective implementation of a balanced literacy program. Classrooms were equipped with a wide range of reading materials. The availability of leveled books in a variety of genres ensured that students could find reading materials that met their abilities, diverse backgrounds, and interests. Both fiction and nonfiction materials were available for students to read. In these schools, instructional time was valued, with interruptions kept to a minimum. Parental engagement and involvement was a top priority. These schools developed a caring and nurturing school climate where students felt safe and respected. They developed an environment where students knew their teachers believed in their ability to succeed.

Changing the pattern of low student achievement is not achieved solely through resources and professional development. A culture of change must be established that mobilizes the passion and commitment of principals, teachers, schools boards, and parents to improve the learning of all students and close the achievement gap. What the OFIP strategy proved was that with focused attention, establishing a few key priorities, and working collaboratively as a team, schools can achieve continuous improvement and reach new heights in student achievement.

Communication and Collaboration

Another key aspect of the Ontario strategy was engaging all stakeholders as the elementary school improvement strategy was developed. Dr. Avis Glaze, the CEO of the Secretariat, traveled throughout the province to discuss the improvement strategy with directors (superintendents) of education, parent groups, teachers' unions, trustee associations, and various other groups. She sought feedback regarding the strategies to be implemented. She instilled a sense of urgency regarding the important work that needed to be done to improve outcomes for all students. The extensive outreach strategy built trust, encouraged two-way communication, and gained support for the improvement agenda. SAOs also gathered input and relayed messages from the field regarding the strategy. Regular newsletters were sent out to update educators about progress being made and next steps. Prior to any new strategies being implemented, the CEO invited directors of education and union groups to focus meetings to discuss the initiatives and gather feedback. The Ministry also established a literacy and numeracy working table that consisted of a wide range of organizations (e.g., principals' associations, teachers' union, supervisory officers' associations, support staff unions, parent groups, etc.). This group met regularly to discuss current issues, solve problems collaboratively, monitor progress, and provide feedback regarding the strategy. Accountability and transparency were hallmarks of elementary reform.

The Importance of Data

Using data effectively to inform the provincial improvement strategy was one of the founding principles of the Secretariat. The analysis of provincial assessments was critical to informing reform efforts. The development, administering, and reporting of provincial assessments are the responsibility of an independent agency, EQAO. The Secretariat made extensive use of EQAO data not only to inform strategic decisions and initiatives but also to support the SAOs' professional dialogue in the field and to focus their work in partnership with districts and schools. Data were used to track progress, identify areas for improvement, and inform the literacy and numeracy strategy.

At no time did the Secretariat use data to rank or penalize schools; its staff made a conscious decision that there would be no such ranking. In fact, one of the innovations of the Secretariat was the creation of a data technology tool known as Ontario Statistical Neighbours so that similar schools could learn from one another. This meant that schools that were achieving at high levels could share their promising practices with lower-performing schools that shared similar demographic characteristics. Ontario Statistical Neighbours is an innovative tool that enabled the Secretariat to access school performance, program, and contextual data. The tool empowered staff at the Secretariat to explore school data such as percentages of students living in low-income households, students whose first language learned at home was different than the language of instruction, and students with special education needs. It also included other school characteristics and demographic information in the analysis. This tool helped the province identify performance trends, such as schools showing significant improvement in a wide range of contexts, including challenging circumstances. This tool was also used to identify schools that became part of the OFIP program. The Ontario Statistical Neighbours tool was specifically designed so that schools could not be ranked. It was intended as a tool to assist with capacity building and providing supports where needed most. It also removed excuses for low performance.

Not all jurisdictions have access to technology such as the Secretariat's Ontario Statistical Neighbours, but they do have a wide range of data available for their use. Gathering and examining statistics such as graduation rates, attendance records, suspension rates, school office referrals, high school credit completion, report card grades, underperforming groups of students, and large-scale assessment results, to name a few, can help identify trends, areas of strengths, and areas in need of improvement. Bringing staff together to discuss the trends and issues, as well as possible solutions, is the first step in the improvement journey.

Integrating Technology Across the Curriculum

Technology has been a powerful tool for teachers to incorporate into their instructional practice. Across Ontario, teachers have integrated technology throughout the curriculum. All schools in Ontario provide access to technology in various forms for their students. Students are learning to become responsible digital citizens and to use the Internet and other multimedia resources for research, connecting with other students around the world, completion of assignments, problem solving, and a range of other tasks. Teachers have been provided with a breadth of learning opportunities to assist them in incorporating technology into their teaching repertoire. The use of technology helps teachers to differentiate their instruction to meet the unique needs of their students. For example, students with special education needs can greatly benefit from the use of adaptive technology. Using a range of technologies can provide teachers with a variety of tools to make their classrooms more inclusive. Technologies such as voice-to-text software, spelling and grammar check, publishing software, tools for organizing thoughts, and drill and practice software can be helpful to all students, not just those with disabilities. While Ontario continues to stress the importance of integrating technology into the curriculum, it was not looked on as the silver bullet to improving student achievement. The foundation of Ontario's elementary improvement strategy was to strengthen classroom instruction. Technology is a tool, but it will only be an effective tool if coupled with high-quality instruction.

Professional Accountability

As educators, we must hold ourselves to the highest level of accountability to our students—after all, we hold their future in our hands. In Ontario, both external and internal measures of student achievement are used to monitor progress. Ontario participates in national and international assessments such as Trends in International Mathematics and Science Study (TIMSS), Progress in International Reading Literacy Study (PIRLS), Program for International Student Assessment (PISA), and the Pan-Canadian Assessment Program. In addition, provincial assessment (EQAO) and school-level data are used to measure student achievement. The message is that there should be multiple measures of achievement rather than a reliance on one tool.

The ultimate form of accountability occurs when professionals engage in self-assessment and are willing to take steps to bring about improvement. As discussed in Chapter 3, Ontario developed the School Effectiveness Framework, which was initially designed for elementary schools but is now used in high schools as well. Schools used this tool to conduct self-assessments.

A school self-assessment answers a number of important questions:

- Where are we now and how are we doing?
- What do our data tell us?
- Who are the students who are underperforming?
- What are our strengths?
- What is the greatest area of need for all students to be successful?
- What actions will we take to ensure continuous improvement?
- How will we know if we have been successful?

Self-assessment improves schools by encouraging the school community to be more proactive in monitoring its own progress. Throughout Ontario, schools are now conducting self-assessments to determine their effectiveness in improving student achievement. This process has resulted in school staff taking greater ownership for improvement efforts and the success of all students. It has taken professional accountability to a higher level.

Summary

In Ontario, it was recognized that to improve graduation rates, it was necessary to strengthen education in the foundational elementary school years. The strategies that were implemented by the Literacy and Numeracy Secretariat resulted not only in higher achievement but also in narrowing gaps. In Ontario, excellence and equity go hand in hand. As a province, we have demonstrated that results can be achieved without alienating our teachers and principals, and without imposing punitive approaches and negative sanctions. We rejected the reliance of some jurisdictions on the ranking of schools.

For change to happen and be sustained, it is critical to have ownership at all levels. Relying solely on top-down approaches has not proven to be effective in the long term. The Secretariat's approach was to work alongside districts and schools, providing a range of supports and capacity building. We encouraged educators to take ownership for their own improvement efforts. We eschewed the one-size-fits-all mentality and provided supports to meet the varying needs of districts and boards. We provided both positive pressure and targeted support to districts and schools to ensure that students received a high-quality elementary school education that would position them for success in high school.

How to Re-Create These Strategies

In Ontario, we recognize that we must be relentless in our quest for continuous improvement in student achievement. Progress is monitored continuously, and revisions are made to the strategy as needed. Improvement efforts must be a continuous and cyclical process of analysis, planning, and implementation designed to enhance student achievement measurably over time. The following is a series of considerations when developing large-scale improvement efforts.

Fundamental Beliefs

The foundation for reform efforts in Ontario rested with the belief that all students can achieve at high levels when provided with high-quality instruction and given appropriate supports and time. There was also a deep belief that early childhood learning is critical to future success. It is essential to instill a sense of urgency in all those responsible for educating our children and to rekindle their sense of moral responsibility to help all students achieve. Building the capacity for improvement is foundational to large-scale reform.

Political Elements

Political and educational leaders need to build partnerships and collaborate with all stakeholders to garner support for change. Shame and blame tactics do not work! Policies and practices must be reviewed and revised where necessary in support of improvement goals. Budget decisions need to be driven by identified student achievement priorities. Share research with policy makers that demonstrate that strategies such as early childhood development have a positive impact on student achievement. Work with professional and community associations to bring attention to areas in need of improvement and to garner support. Be prepared to discuss what may have to be discontinued to finance new initiatives.

Key Strategies

- Ensure dialogue and engagement with all stakeholders.
- Provide high quality early childhood learning opportunities.
- Reduce primary class size.
- Establish a few key priorities and stay the course.
- Establish high expectations and set ambitious targets.
- Ensure every child has a strong foundation in literacy and numeracy skills.
- Build capacity by investing in, supporting, and developing your people.
- Provide the necessary resources to support instruction and leadership.
- Reject the one-size-fits-all approach.
- Provide targeted supports for schools and students who are struggling.
- Conduct assessments of district and school effectiveness.
- Support community outreach and engagement.
- Ensure international comparability.

Reaching Teachers

High-quality instruction is critical to student success. Providing the resources and professional learning needed for the effective implementation of high-impact strategies is key. Teachers have varying needs regarding their professional learning; therefore, educational systems need to diversify their approach and engage teachers in discussions about their learning needs. They also need a clear vision of system priorities and time to implement required strategies. When teachers are included in the improvement process, they take ownership for the results.

Reaching School Districts

For states or provinces to engage school districts in reform measures, they need to encourage dialogue and ongoing discussion regarding the improvement strategy. Ongoing communication and consultation results in best thinking. When planning professional learning opportunities or providing resources, state or provincial leaders need to work collaboratively with local districts to ensure the local context and

(continued)

(continued)

needs are considered. To make change happen and to have improvement strategies deeply embedded, it is necessary to recognize that the strategy must be properly supported at all levels of the system.

Resources and Supports

The reality in today's world is that most educational systems face many financial challenges. Therefore, for any improvement strategy to succeed, policy makers must make some difficult decisions regarding budget allocations. That means that those things that do not move the system forward in meeting identified student achievement priorities must be dropped, or their funding reduced. We need to make sure that educators have the professional learning supports they need and the classroom resources to get the job done. It doesn't necessarily mean more money, but rather using the resources we currently have in new and more effective ways.

References

Barber, M., & Mourshed, M. (2007). *How the world's best-performing school systems come out on top.* New York: McKinsey & Company.

Barber, M., & Mourshed, M. (2009). *Shaping the future: How good education systems can become great in the decade ahead.* New York: McKinsey & Company.

Berrill, D. (2009, October). Try literacy tutoring first. *What works? research into practice.* Toronto, ON: The Literacy and Numeracy Secretariat, Ontario Ministry of Education. Retrieved from http://www.edu.gov.on.ca/eng/literacynumeracy/inspire/research/WW_Literacy_Tutors.pdf

Campbell, C., Comper, J., & Winton, S. (2007, February). Successful and sustainable practices for raising student achievement in literacy and numeracy. *Changing Perspectives,* 31–36.

Campbell, C., Fullan, M., & Glaze, A. (2006). *Unlocking potential for learning: Effective district-wide strategies to raise student achievement in literacy and numeracy.* Toronto: Ontario Ministry of Education.

Canadian Language and Literacy Research Network (CLLRNet). (2009, Spring). *The impact of the Literacy and Numeracy Secretariat: Changes in Ontario's education system* (Report for the Ontario Ministry of Education). Toronto, ON: Author. www.edu.gov.on.ca/eng/document/reports/OME_Report09_EN.pdf

Carbo, R. (2008). Strategies for increasing achievement in reading. In R. W. Cole (Ed.), *Educating everybody's children: Diverse teaching strategies for diverse learners* (pp. 98–112). Alexandria, VA: ASCD.

Curran, R., Balfanz, R., & Herzog, L. (2007, October). An early warning system. *Educational Leadership, 65*(2), 28–33.

Education Quality and Accountability Office (EQAO). (2011). *Highlights of the provincial achievement results 2010–2011.* Toronto, ON: Author. Retrieved from http://www.eqao.com/pdf_e/11/EQAO_PJ9Highlights_2011.pdf

Field, S., Kuczera, M., & Pont, B. (2007). *No more failures: Ten steps to equality in education.* Paris: OECD.

Fullan, M. (2005). *Leadership and sustainability.* Thousand Oaks, CA: Corwin.

Hammond, C., Linton, D., Smink, J., & Drew, S. (2007, May). *Drop out risk factors and exemplary programs: A technical report.* Clemson, SC: National Dropout Prevention Center/Network. Retrieved from http://maec.ceee.gwu.edu/files/Dropout_Risk_Factors_and_Exemplary_Programs_Clemson_2007.pdf

Hopkins, D. (2005, August). *Every school a great school* (IARTV Seminar Series Paper No. 146). Victoria, Australia: IARTV.

Klinger, D., Shulha, L. A., & Wade-Woolley, L. (2009, November). *Towards an understanding of gender differences in literacy achievement* (Research Bulletin 5). Toronto, ON: Education Quality and Accountability Office. Retrieved from http://www.eqao.com/Research/pdf/E/FINAL_ENGLISH_Gender_Gap_Report_As_of_May_11_2010.pdf

Leithwood, K., Seashore Louis, K., Anderson, S., & Wahlstrom, K. (2004, September). *How leadership influences student learning: A review of research for the learning from leadership project.* New York: The Wallace Foundation/Center for Applied Research and Educational Improvement, University of Minnesota/Ontario Institute for Studies in Education.

Lopez, S. (2011, October). The highs and lows of student engagement. *Phi Delta Kappan, 93*(2), 72–73.

McCain, M., & Mustard, F. (1999). *Reversing the real brain drain: Early years study: Final report.* Toronto: Ontario Children's Secretariat.

McCain, M., Mustard, F., & McCuaig, K. (2011). *Early years study 3: Making decisions, taking action.* Toronto, ON: Margaret and Wallace McCain Family Foundation.

McCain, M., Mustard, F., & Shanker, S. (2007). *Early years study 2: Putting science into action.* Toronto, ON: Council for Early Childhood Development.

McKinsey & Company. (2009, April). *The economic impact of the achievement gap in America's schools.* New York: Author. Retrieved from https://mckinseyonsociety.com/downloads/reports/Education/achievement_gap_report.pdf

Mourshed, M., Chijioke, C., & Barber, M. (2010). *How the world's most improved school systems keep getting better.* New York: McKinsey & Company.

Ontario Ministry of Education. (2006). *Target setting and improvement planning.* (2006). Toronto: Queen's Printer for Ontario.

Ontario Ministry of Education. (2011). *Ontario schools: Kindergarten to Grade 12—policy and program requirements.* Toronto: Queen's Printer for Ontario.

Ontario Ministry of Education, Literacy and Numeracy Secretariat. (2007). *Schools on the move (Lighthouse Program).* Toronto: Queen's Printer for Ontario. Retrieved from http://www.edu.gov.on.ca/eng/literacynumeracy/onthemove2007.pdf

Ontario Ministry of Education, Literacy and Numeracy Secretariat. (2008, March). *Non-fiction writing for the junior student* (Capacity Building Series, Secretariat Special Edition No. 5). Toronto: Queen's Printer for Ontario. Retrieved from http://www.edu.gov.on.ca/eng/literacynumeracy/inspire/research/non_fiction_writing.pdf

Reeves, D. (2002, March–April). Six principles of effective accountability: Accountability-based reforms should lead to better teaching and learning-period. *Harvard Education Letter, 18*(2). Retrieved from www.hepg.org/hel/article/208

Schmoker, M. (2011). *Focus: Elevating the essentials to radically improve student learning.* Alexandria, VA: ASCD.

Snow, D. (2003). *Classroom strategies for helping at-risk students.* Denver, CO: McRel.

Willms, J. D., Frieson, S., & Milton, P. (2009). *What did you do in school today? Transforming classrooms through social, academic and intellectual engagement: First national report.* Toronto, ON: Canadian Education Association.

5

High-Impact Strategies for Secondary Schools

The challenge of transforming secondary schools has been a long-standing focus of educators and governments in Ontario. Responding to this challenge in the past decade has led the province to consider fundamental changes in what constitutes success and in the means by which educators strive to ensure this success in the educational context. Significantly, it is about how to change opportunities for students and to move toward the evolution of traditional practices to improve support for all students. This will create the conditions for success within and beyond our secondary schools.

Leadership Is the Key

To address the challenge of undertaking large-scale, systemic change for Grades 7 through 12, the Ministry of Education in Ontario first established a unique leadership network across the province, sending a clear message about the fundamental importance of the new student success strategy. In every school district and authority in the province, a new position was established for a student success leader (SSL), a senior administrator whose sole responsibility was to oversee the allocation of funding associated with the strategy and to lead the implementation of specific initiatives within that strategy. These leaders were connected directly to both the executive lead (director) of each school board and to Ministry staff and were the key contacts for all implementation initiatives for the student success strategy.

In addition to the SSL, the Ministry of Education also created the position of the student success teacher (SST). Policy/Program Memorandum 137 defines this person as a teacher designated to

> know and track the progress of students at risk of not graduating; support school-wide efforts to improve outcomes for students struggling with the secondary curriculum; re-engage early school leavers; provide direct support/instruction to these students in order to improve student achievement, retention, and transitions; and work with parents and the community to support student success. (Ontario Ministry of Education, 2005)

These teachers also formed, along with school administration, guidance, and special education staff, the Student Success team in every Ontario secondary school. This team directs the implementation of the Student Success strategy and leads efforts related to the strategy in secondary schools.

The Pillars of Student Success

The change imperative in Ontario secondary schools has focused on three main themes: building foundational skills in literacy and numerical literacy, including a focus on instructional practices; providing a more explicit and rich menu of programs and pathways; and focusing on the individual well-being of students as a precursory foundation for achievement. The vehicle for implementing strategies in these areas has been the Student Success/Learning to 18 Strategy. The strategy has focused on these three themes through the introduction of four pillars of student success: literacy, numeracy, program pathways, and community culture and caring. An investigation of the background leading to the development of the initiative and of each pillar will serve to illustrate how the Ministry was able to work collaboratively with school boards across Ontario to raise the provincial graduation rate from 68% to 82% in only seven years, and how the percentage of students reading and writing at a ninth-grade level of literacy was raised to 85% for the province.

Literacy

In 2003, the final report of an expert panel of educators, *Think Literacy Success*, was released to school districts. This report frames the literacy strategy by stating that

> *all* educators have a role in ensuring that students graduate with the essential literacy skills for life. It calls on teachers, school administrators, families, community members, super-intendents, and directors to work together to ensure student success . . . embedding high literacy standards and effective literacy practices across the curriculum, from Kindergarten to Grade 12. (Ontario Ministry of Education, 2003, p. 11)

The literacy strategy was intended to attain this goal in Ontario schools and consisted of training and literacy support materials based on the *Think Literacy Success* document, as well as a number of supports for educators. Overall, the literacy strategy focused on teacher training and resource development for the Ontario Secondary School Literacy Test (OSSLT) and Ontario Secondary School Literacy Course (OSSLC), on the provision of targeted resources for males who, the data indicated, struggled more with literacy than did female students, and cross-curricular literacy plans. Professional learning opportunities in the teaching of reading and writing in secondary education, and teacher-moderated marking sessions were developed to build capacity within classrooms.

The Ontario Secondary School Literacy Course

The OSSLC was also introduced as a support for students who had been unsuccessful in passing the provincial literacy test, the OSSLT, which was made a requirement of graduation for students entering Grade 9 in the 2000–2001 school year. The course consists of seventeen key expectations, all of which must be demonstrated by students to attain this credit.

Targeted Resources

One area of support resources was the identification and provision of male-focused and high-interest, relevant resources for students at a variety of literacy levels. Through the provision of these resources, students who were struggling with literacy could work with materials that were age-appropriate with a high-interest factor but that were created at a vocabulary level appropriate to the students' needs.

Teacher Professional Learning

Many districts also focused on the explicit training of secondary school teachers in the teaching of specific reading and writing skill sets outside of a curricular framework. This work had been traditionally reserved for teachers in elementary schools but was deemed necessary to best assist students facing literacy challenges in these areas.

Moderated Marking

A key activity that gained currency through the literacy strategy was the practice of having groups of teachers work together to evaluate student work, thereby improving consensus regarding the meaning of various levels of achievement and the consistency with which written work was evaluated against a common set of criteria, usually expressed in a rubric. This marking was often associated with the OSSLC or with a practice literacy test administered in Grade 9, the first year of secondary school. This allowed teachers to identify specific students who would benefit from additional support in the time leading up to the actual test in Grade 10 and the areas in which they needed assistance.

Cross-Curricular Literacy

Cross-curricular literacy simply refers to the practice of applying common teaching strategies and focus on literacy across all or multiple subject areas. This approach required teachers to work collaboratively to define the areas of focus or literacy strategies they would emphasize across the curriculum and then monitor the results. When combined with specific knowledge of student needs based on practice literacy test results or other diagnostic assessments of literacy—many districts designed their own—these strategies resulted in gains for students writing the literacy test, the principle means whereby students attain the graduation requirement in literacy.

The Secondary School Literacy Strategy

How to Re-Create These Strategies

Just as Ontario faced a challenge of helping students to meet a provincial literacy standard, literacy challenges can be identified and quantified in most school districts. The following is a series of considerations for addressing these challenges, learning from the Ontario model.

Fundamental Beliefs

The underpinning principles of the literacy strategy center on the belief that students can attain literacy skills at Grade 9 levels and that literacy can be taught and learned effectively with the proper strategies.

Key Strategies

- A clear and explicitly communicated framework for success, including fundamental beliefs and principles, intended outcomes, and supports
- Evidence of need as illustrated by clear, student-based data to shape the development of the overall approach so that it addresses the specific needs of the district
- Resources targeted at attaining the stated outcomes
- Professional learning for teachers at all levels to address literacy instruction across the curriculum and in all grades but with a major focus leading to and including Grade 10

Political Elements

Support of education departments is helpful to align findings and to guide the development of the framework, resources, and strategies.

Reaching Teachers

The engagement of teachers and school administrators is critical in the implementation of any successful educational program. Educators must be supported with a clear vision of the intended outcome of endeavors such as the literacy strategy, an active role and opportunity to apply their experience to the development of the framework, and resources to support work in specific school and classroom plans. Professional learning, resources, and communication are required to implement this strategy successfully.

Reaching School Districts

School districts need to be supported by clear communications and funding plans, training schedules, and the resources necessary to allow teachers and administrators to access the knowledge, skills training, and tools necessary to implement the strategies outlined here.

Resources and Supports

Reading and writing instruction training, appropriately leveled resources, and funding to support the objectives of the framework generated for the school or district are necessary to successfully implement this strategy.

Numeracy

In 2004, the expert panel report *Leading Math Success* was released to SSLs and school districts. The report states that its purpose is "to help create a brighter future for Ontario adolescents who are currently at risk of leaving high school without the mathematics skills and understanding they need to reach their full potential in the twenty-first century" (Ontario Ministry of Education, 2004, p. 9). Numerical literacy continues to be an area of focus for school boards and districts across Ontario, and the recommendations of the expert panel are still in force in this pursuit.

The numeracy strategy resulted from a strong partnership between the Student Success branches and the curriculum branch of the Ministry of Education, and focuses on improving opportunities for students to acquire and demonstrate their learning of mathematics. It is supported by materials based on the *Leading Math Success* document and on subsequent Ministry initiatives such as Targeted Implementation and Planning Supports (TIPS) and TIPS for Revised Mathematics (TIPS4RM).

A variety of related projects and research has been implemented to assist with a focus on mathematics and numeracy instruction, including the Growing Accessible Interactive Networked Supports, Professional Resources and Instruction for Mathematics Educators and Programming Remediation and Intervention for Students in Mathematics projects, Math Critical Learning Instructional Paths Supports, and specific funding for differentiated instruction for mathematics. Additional support came from colleges through the College Math Project (2012) and research reports such as the Curriculum Implementation in Intermediate Mathematics (2007). Both the literacy and numeracy initiatives have benefited from the provision of Learning Opportunity Grant money being available to fund after-school programs for students.

Areas of Focus

The numeracy strategy focused on professional learning sessions for teachers, structured lesson design, and resource development and application, including technology applications for a variety of student learning styles. Varied projects and pilots for the math strategy implementation were funded, and resources were developed for use in the classroom. In the 2010–2011 school year, a group of mathematics educators and researchers gathered to further map out the strategy and to discuss recommendations for additional improvements. The use of collaborative inquiry—the process by which a group of educators engages in the joint consideration of student work with a goal of identifying and

addressing areas of learning need for specific students in a classroom—
has become an increasingly central support in mathematics instruction
in the province.

The Secondary School Numeracy Strategy

How to Re-Create These Strategies

While Ontario still faces a challenge with respect to improvement of student learning in mathematics, strong steps and gains are being made in most school districts. The following is a series of considerations for addressing these challenges, based on the Ontario model.

Fundamental Beliefs

The principles of the numeracy strategy center on the belief that assisting teachers to become more comfortable with differentiated practices to meet specific student learning needs will continue to facilitate the development of appropriate strategies for student success.

Key Strategies

- A clear and explicitly communicated framework for success, including fundamental beliefs and principles, intended outcomes, and supports
- The consideration of individual student learning and the subsequent identification of specific learning needs to be addressed with appropriate instructional strategies
- Resources targeted at attaining the stated outcomes
- Professional learning for teachers at all levels to assist with the process of collaborative inquiry, engagement strategies, and the development of new lesson structures and classroom practices

Political Elements

Support of education departments is helpful to align findings and to guide the development of the framework, resources, and strategies.

Reaching Teachers

Engaging teachers and school administrators is critical in the implementation of any successful educational program. Educators must be supported with a clear vision of the intended outcomes, such as those identified in the the numeracy strategy; an active role and opportunity for teachers to apply their experience to the development of the framework; and resources to support work in specific school and classroom plans. Professional learning, resources, and communication are required to successfully implement this strategy.

(Continued)

(Continued)

Reaching School Districts

School districts need to be supported by clear communications and funding plans, training schedules, and the resources necessary to allow teachers and administrators to access the knowledge, skills training, and tools to implement the strategies outlined here.

Resources and Supports

Specific mathematics instruction training, manipulative resources, diagnostic tools, the development of professional learning teams, and funding to support the objectives are necessary to implement this strategy successfully.

Instructional Practice

Although it is not technically a "pillar" of the Student Success strategy, the focus on instructional practice has grown from the pillars of Literacy and Numeracy. Any improvement in education ultimately needs to happen in the classroom. The teaching–learning relationship between individual students and their teacher is, at the moment, the defining characteristic of the educational process. Whether students and teachers make a connection on some level that allows those students to better unlock their learning potential is a critical component in systemic educational improvement.

The explicit focus on instructional practice for secondary schools has been taken up in varying degrees in schools and school districts across Ontario. This variability has required increasingly precise, specific, and targeted approaches to building instructional leadership capacity, using evidence, developing frameworks and tools for assessment, and an increasing effort to support teacher creativity within a common framework of resources and guiding principles. Outside the efforts in literacy and numeracy, four main areas of focus in these endeavors have been

- using collaborative inquiry planning processes,
- focusing on differentiated instruction with supporting resources,
- connecting more strongly to address the special needs of some students, and
- reconsidering assessment and evaluation practices.

Collaborative Inquiry Planning Processes

As schools and school districts considered the challenges of improvement in a system that has been recognized as one of the five best in the world (Mourshed, Chijioke, & Barber, 2010), and as they considered the data and evidence that were increasingly both available and abundant, the need for common frameworks became critical. The entrance into a collective consideration of problems of practice, focused on the use of (often observational) evidence and the use of research-informed practices to devise strategies to address these issues, is termed *collaborative inquiry.* Schools had used a school improvement plan process for years in Ontario in varying degrees to build continuity within districts, but there was no overarching provincial framework with which to work. In 2005, the Literacy and Numeracy Secretariat introduced a school effectiveness framework (SEF) for elementary schools (Government of Ontario, 2010b). The framework would evolve into a broad self-assessment tool for all schools in the province in the 2008–2009 school year. This framework focused on large-scale educational processes such as assessment and evaluation, which were relevant in all grades, and provided indicators and evidence exemplars for use at all levels of the educational system. In 2008, the Student Achievement Division of the Ministry of Education introduced a universal Board Improvement Plan for Student Achievement template that included an extensive assessment tool to help guide school districts in their reflection for planning.

These supports and frameworks were predominantly based at the system and school levels, but they formalized a process that could be replicated in the more intimate environment of the classroom. In 2009, the Student Success strategy introduced a Professional Learning Cycle to teachers in the intermediate (Grades 7–10) and senior (Grades 11 and 12) divisions. This collaborative inquiry process, illustrated in Figure 5.1, is a simple, often represented process that can be applied to reflective practice at any level in the educational system from the classroom to the political scale. This can assist educators in becoming explicit and intentional in their practice.

Differentiated Instruction and Supporting Resources

A great deal of research, from Gardner's (1983) theory of multiple intelligences through the work of Tomlinson (1999), Nunley (2001), and others has focused on the benefits of knowing more about and responding in explicit and meaningful ways to the diverse learning needs of the

Figure 5.1 The Professional Learning Cycle

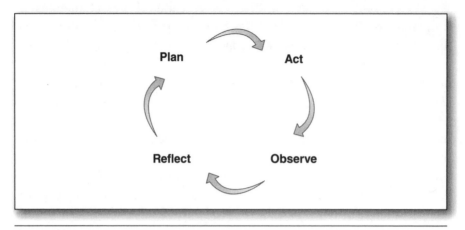

Source: Ministry of Education for Ontario. (2010). *School Effectiveness Framework: A support for school improvement and student success.* Toronto, Canada: Queen's Printer for Ontario.

individual students in any given classroom. The consideration of student and teacher profiles in any manner of areas such as readiness to learn, prior knowledge, learning style, or multiple intelligences can profoundly change how teachers approach the task of facilitating the student's acquisition of knowledge, information, skills, and understanding in ways that allow them to best internalize and apply that learning. Such differentiation can occur in areas of lesson content, in the processes available to students to access learning, and in the products they are asked to produce as a demonstration of that learning. Differentiation of instruction based on an understanding of the student's need through collected and observed evidence helps educators to see new ways of creating catalysts for students to engage with their learning. They can also expand their own approaches to instruction that extend beyond their own preferred teaching and learning styles.

Connections to Students With Special Education Needs

One form of differentiation that has existed for some time in Ontario and that is critical to reducing achievement gaps within and among groups of students is the process of assessing areas of special need for students with exceptionalities of a developmental or cognitive processing nature, and establishing and implementing strategies to address these particular exceptionalities in addition to other learning needs. In Ontario, this work has been characterized as "special education" and encompasses a wide spectrum of exceptionalities, from students who have significant developmental delays that place them far behind their age cohort with respect to their cognitive function, to students with very high measured intelligence quotients that place them in the top few percentiles of the population with regard to this measurement of intellectual capacity. The importance of this focus is in recognizing the specific nature of the exceptionalities the student is facing, creating a series of research-based strategies and implementing those strategies to mitigate for exceptionality and optimize the learning opportunities for each student.

Assessment and Evaluation

The continual assessment of students accompanied by the requisite changes in teaching approaches, strategies, and practices to address the learning needs identified by these assessments is a hallmark of effective teaching practice. The Ontario experience has included the revision in 2008 of the assessment and evaluation policy document and the release of *Growing Success* (Government of Ontario, 2010a). This is a document that sets the framework for all assessment and evaluation practices and policies from school entry to the completion of secondary school. One of the key areas of focus for the document and for effective assessment practice is the delineation of three types of assessment: assessment *for* learning, assessment *as* learning, and assessment *of* learning, or evaluation. The distinction is an important one as it demonstrates a reinforcement of the concept that assessment of students in a classroom has a far broader scope than simply making a judgment of their work and assigning a value to that judgment to form the basis for a final grade. By embedding assessment for and as learning into the assessment policies, Ontario signaled the importance to effective instruction of self-, peer, and teacher assessments of student understanding and the capacity to demonstrate key curriculum expectations prior to evaluation—a time during which instructional steps may still be taken to enhance learning and further optimize the student's capacity to demonstrate key learning expectations.

One important distinction when considering assessment and evaluation practices is the one between large-scale standardized assessments and less formalized assessment tools and activities. When educators conduct an assessment of student learning needs to better refine their differentiation of instruction for their students, they will use a wide variety of tools with a focus that reflects the nature of the learning needs most commonly found in the subject area or type of learning in which they seek to engage their students. These less formal tools, which often take but a few minutes to administer (red, yellow, or green card self-assessments of understanding; brief quiz-like assessments of major concepts; diagnostics of prior learning before entering new subject matter; etc.), are much more prevalent and perhaps carry a greater daily facility for the educator than the larger-scale standardized assessments (such as the Diagnostic Reading Assessment, Comprehension Attitude Strategies Interest, or Education Quality and Accountability Office tests) that may be administered. The distinction is important when discussing assessment, as often it is equated to these types of larger-scale standardized tools as opposed to the more nimble and immediate assessments that teachers make of their students on an ongoing basis in the daily practice of teaching.

The Instructional Practice Strategy

How to Re-Create These Strategies

Ontario's journey into a strategic, focused, and consistent set of strategies in instructional practice has already provided a foundation for teacher creativity and instructional leadership to flourish. The following is a series of considerations for addressing these challenges, learning from the Ontario model.

Fundamental Beliefs

The underpinning principles of the instructional practice strategy is that excellent teaching and learning practice exists within and beyond the classrooms of Ontario and that the mobilization of knowledge about these practices and the engagement of teachers in the examination and ongoing evolution of practice will lead to greater student engagement and achievement for the learners in the 21st century.

Key Strategies

- A framework for the consideration of instructional practices
- Vehicles for the explicit organization and consideration of instructional practice
- Key resources and supports for capacity building in school, system, and classroom leaders to create and sustain a culture of continuous collaborative inquiry

Political Elements

Support of education departments is helpful to align findings and to guide the development of the framework, resources, and strategies.

Reaching Teachers

The engagement of teachers and school administrators is critical in the implementation of any successful educational program. These educators must be supported with a clear vision of the intended outcome of endeavors such as the instructional practice strategy, an active role, and opportunity to apply their experience to the development of the framework and resources to support work in specific school and classroom plans. Professional learning, resources and communication are required to successfully implement this strategy.

Reaching School Districts

School districts need to be supported by clear communications and funding plans, training schedules, and the resources necessary to allow teachers and administrators to access the knowledge, skills training, and tools to implement the strategies outlined here.

Resources and Supports

Specific instructional practice and leadership capacity-building training, appropriate resources, and the development of professional learning teams and funding to support the objectives of the framework generated for the school or district are necessary to successfully implement this strategy.

Program Pathways

Perhaps one of the key defining characteristics of the Student Success strategy in Ontario was the explicit focus on improving course and program offerings for students who were not bound for a postsecondary destination in the university pathway. The concept of creating specific pathways for students bound for apprenticeship, college, or the workplace was not new or unique to Ontario schools. The combination of an explicit focus along with a guiding expert panel report, *Building Pathways for Success Grades 7–12* (Government of Ontario, 2003), helped to frame this element of the strategy and allow for the implementation of a variety of tools to assist schools. This included expanded co-op credits, specialist high skills major programs, dual credit programs, the School College Work Initiative, lighthouse projects, and broader college partnerships.

Expanded Co-Op Credits

In 2008, the Ontario Ministry of Education changed policies regarding the use of co-operative education courses, the name for courses in which students spend time in a workplace setting that is related to a course of study they have completed or are completing in the school setting. This form of experiential education provides students with a greater degree of relevant application of learned skills, develops new skills, and provides valuable experience in a work sector in which they may have an interest after completing schooling. The policy change recognized to a greater degree the importance of these courses by making it possible for them to contribute to a student's list of compulsory graduation credits. This policy change signaled the value in the greater preparation of students for the workplace after and, in so doing, also served as a statement on the value of the workplace and apprenticeship destinations.

Specialist High Skills Major

In 2006, the Ministry started a new program for organizing curriculum and other specific prerequisites that would allow students to qualify for a new type of certification in addition to their Ontario Secondary School Diploma (graduation certificate): the Specialist High Skills Major (SHSM). The concept of the SHSM was the creation of a program at the school and community level that consisted of a specific economic sector focus and included five key elements: a bundle of eight to ten credits with the sector focus, specialized units called *contextualized learning activities* within courses (i.e., mathematics or English) in which applications to the sector were specifically made (i.e., tree stand density calculations in mathematics courses in a forestry SHSM), experiential learning opportunities (two co-operative education credits at a minimum), industry-recognized certifications as prescribed by Ministry documents, and the use of the Ontario Skills Passport, an employer-completed record of skills that could be used in future employment by the student. These programs, designed by schools but assessed by the Ministry for compliance with the program requirements, gave a strong focus and relevance to programming for students seeking eventual employment through any of the four major destination pathways: apprenticeship, college, university, and direct entry to the workplace.

Dual Credit Program and School College Work

A further means of strengthening programming for students who were not bound for universities involved a connection between the Ministry and the Council of Directors of Education and a program called the School to College to Work Initiative (SCWI). In particular, in 2007, the concept of a *dual credit* was introduced. These were special courses in which students received instruction at a community college and were able to gain credit both at the college (for future application toward a diploma program) and at the secondary school (for application toward their Ontario Secondary School Diploma). These programs are considered to be largely responsible for subsequent increases in the rate of students attending community college, especially those students who attend directly after graduation from secondary school.

Lighthouse Projects

From 2004 to 2008, the Ministry opened funding to district school boards to allow them to apply for short-term support for programs they felt would further their ability to support students at risk of not graduating or who were in risk situations. These differentiated projects were intended to allow boards to identify and address conditions of local need and to provide the Ministry with insights into successful practices to assist students. Many of the projects funded included support for students seeking postsecondary opportunities in a variety of postsecondary destinations, including apprenticeship, college, and the direct entry to the workplace.

College Partnerships

Partnerships with community colleges in Ontario have always been important in creating opportunities for students to understand, explore, and eventually enter the programs offered by these institutions. Prior to the development of the SCWI, many colleges actively sought partnerships with districts to help students to take courses associated with diploma programs at the college. Partnerships with colleges were particularly aimed at apprenticeship and college pathway students, and helped many students to "see" themselves at college and thereby act on meeting entry requirements.

The Secondary School Program Pathways Strategy

How to Re-Create These Strategies

Pathways support relies on a clearly communicated statement of value for all postsecondary destinations supported by funding and program support to create strong programs for students in that destination pathway.

Fundamental Beliefs

The underpinning principles of the pathways strategy center on the belief that despite being the pathway that most educators have taken, the university pathway

(Continued)

(Continued)

cannot be held as superior to other destination pathways, and that high-quality programs in all pathways must be developed and supported.

Key Strategies

- A clear and explicitly communicated framework for success, including fundamental beliefs and principles, intended outcomes, and supports
- The explicit funding support for program development, implementation, and sustainability in all destination pathways
- Resources targeted at attaining the stated outcomes
- Professional learning for teachers at all levels to assist with the process of developing, implementing, and sustaining these programs.

Political Elements

Support and funding for program, communication, and policy development to facilitate effective pathways programming for all postsecondary destinations.

Reaching Teachers

The engagement of teachers and school administrators is critical in the implementation of any successful educational program. These educators must be supported with a clear vision of the intended outcome of endeavors, such as the pathways strategy, and be given a real opportunity to actively apply their experience to the development of the framework and resources to support work in specific school and classroom plans. Professional learning, resources, and communication are required to successfully implement this strategy.

Reaching School Districts

School districts need to be supported by clear communications and funding plans, training schedules, and the resources necessary to allow teachers and administrators to access the knowledge and skills training and the tools to implement the strategies outlined here.

Resources and Supports

Specific communication of the vision; planning opportunities that engage the school staff and partner with the broader community, including colleges, employment sector connections, and apprenticeship providers; and funding to support the objectives of the framework are necessary to successfully implement this strategy.

Community, Culture, and Caring

The fourth pillar deals with the nonacademic challenges that often have an incredible bearing on the student's ability to engage in the academic pursuits of education. In this sense, the community, culture, and caring pillar is almost foundational to the other three pillars in that, like Maslow's (1943) hierarchy of needs, the personal preconditions for learning must be met before many students are able to engage in their education. Based largely on the work of Dr. Bruce Ferguson's *Early School Leavers* report (Tilleczek, Ferguson, Boydell, & Rummens, 2005), the title of the pillar incorporates the focus on a broader support system for students and education (community), a realization that the lives of students are diverse and need to be understood to serve those students fully (culture), and the necessity for a caring adult who will mentor, advocate for, and support each individual student (caring). The elements of the strategy focus on targeting specific students for support; the transitions strategy, including the key caring adult; academic interventions like credit recovery; and listening to students, as exemplified by student voice projects.

Related Research

Dr. Bruce Ferguson of the Hospital for Sick Children in Toronto, has partnered with Dr. Kate Tilleczek of Ottawa University and others to author two key reports—*Early School Leavers* (Tilleczek et al., 2005) and *Fresh Starts and False Starts* (Tilleczek et al., 2009)—that have assisted understanding of the perspective of students who have disengaged from education in Ontario and who are transitioning from elementary to secondary school. Dr. Ferguson's summary of the necessary response to the early leaver study has been both simple and profound: Be proactive in helping to reduce and prevent barriers to success; be more understanding of the lived experience of youth, especially where it deviates from that of educators; and be more flexible in helping students address their needs. The report also modeled the practice of listening to the voices of students as a key source of evidence for educational decision making. The transition report similarly focused on student experience and reinforced the importance of the nonacademic experience and culture of the school environment in helping students to be successful. Other work in student engagement, such as that of Willms, Friesen, and Milton (2009), reinforces this message and the importance of the concept of student engagement as a critical precondition for success.

Targeted Students and Precise Practice

The concept of targeting students who struggle is not unique in educational research or practice. Countless studies have been done on selected groups of students and their achievement—be they ethno-cultural, gender, special education needs, achievement levels, course types, or some other criterion-based focus group. The keys to success with any focus of this nature are to remain cognizant of the learning needs of the actual individual students with whom educators are interacting and to respond to those needs through regular assessment and the implementation of research, including proven strategies to address the actual causes of the issues facing these students. The promotion of differentiated instruction, effective assessment (the process of determining what the student learning needs are), and collaborative inquiry into addressing identified learning issues are all promising steps that Ontario has taken to address the issue of differences in student achievement. Greater individualization of knowledge of student need and the development of effective strategies to address the needs is the hallmark of the most effective work in this area.

With respect to community, culture, and caring, this can include the work of the Student Success team and a broader group of teachers who in many schools hold regular conferences to address students in need of support beyond the academic sphere and the nature of that support. The Ministry of Education requests regular reports (titled *Taking Stock*) of students who are at risk of not graduating or who are deemed to be in risk situations, as well as an accounting of some of the strategies used to mitigate the risks facing these students. A study by Willms et al. (2009) indicates that student engagement peaks in elementary school and then declines steadily until the Grade 11, the penultimate grade of secondary school, at which point there is a very modest increase in engagement levels. This engagement is measured by attendance, participation in school organizations (such as clubs and teams), and self-described sense of belonging and intellectual engagement.

Transitions

Part of the targeting strategy in Ontario is to focus on students in transition. While there is an increasing focus on all transitional processes associated with the secondary schooling process (i.e., grade to grade, school to care, and the reverse), the main focus has been on the transition from elementary (Grade 8) to secondary (Grade 9). In this process, SSTs meet with staff from the elementary schools to discuss student profiles and identify students who might benefit from a host of specific interventions, such as a strength- or interest-based timetable, a specific success plan, including special needs, counseling or guidance support, and the explicit assignment of a "caring adult" and sometimes a peer mentor to ensure that the transition to secondary school is as smooth as possible.

Caring Adult

The concept of a caring adult is supported by research from fields of education, youth engagement, volunteer organizations, and mental health that indicates that an adult mentor and advocate is one of the primary drivers of success for young people in transition. This also prevents students in risk situations from experiencing the negative academic consequences that often accompany these situations. Ontario schools have refined this process and often assign staff to specific students to develop a supportive relationship. In the most successful examples, these relationships develop quickly through a natural connection between the student and staff, be it a classroom teacher, counselor, coach, custodian, or secretary, education assistant, or some other adult in the educational community. In several schools, the SST will initially make the connection while this other relationship is developing. These people monitor the student's progress and keep an eye out for any situations or conditions that develop and that may have a negative impact on the student, and then participate in the facilitation of appropriate supports and interventions for that student.

Credit Recovery

One of the interventions that was created to support students in reducing barriers to graduation but that still honors the rigor of the requirements necessary for graduation is credit recovery. Although the principle of credit recovery has been in Ontario education policy since 1999, it was explicitly articulated after 2005. The principle of the intervention is that when students do not demonstrate the Ontario curriculum expectations of a given course to a sufficient degree, they will receive a failing grade and will not be awarded a credit in the course. As Ontario requires thirty credits (eighteen of which are mandated or compulsory courses) for graduation, this represents a significant setback in the path to graduation for the student. When the research (King, Warren, King, Brook, & Kocher 2009) shows that failure of even one course in secondary school significantly increases the chance of not graduating, the importance of recovering failed credits becomes apparent. The repetition of entire courses failed has been and somewhat remains, a common practice in Ontario schools. Credit recovery is a process in which teachers identify which expectations the student did not successfully demonstrate when failing a course, and it is only those expectations that form the focus of the credit remediation process. This reduces the time necessary and allows students to regain multiple failed credits in a time span during which they might only regain one credit if they were to repeat an entire course. In this way, the student can demonstrate the expectations successfully, still complete all of the academic work necessary to allow for legitimate credit granting, and yet not spend an inordinate amount of time completing graduation requirements and developing the hopelessness that often accompanies attempts by older students with lower credit counts to pursue graduation.

Student Voice, Including SPEAK UP

One of the hallmarks of the Ontario strategy for the educational engagement of students is the element of listening to the student voice. While the concept of student government is a popular one in North America, the student voice initiative has a broader mandate of engaging the thoughts of all students, including groups of students who might not normally get a voice in their school. Student voice as described here and as practiced in Ontario schools in the most part refers to the involvement by students in some forms of school change. Schools, bounded by legislation and both government and local policies as they are, are traditionally places in which adults are expected to create and enforce the expectations, limitations, and operating procedures for all school community members. To mitigate the sense of disengagement that this can sometimes create for students participating in the community, many forms of student governments, often modeled on existing adult political structures, have been created in schools. Ontario has even gone so far as to allow a student trustee (elected by other students of the school board) to sit as a trustee at meetings of the school board. This, of course, is student voice at work; the students having a place at the highest tables where decisions are debated and ultimately decided (although the student trustee does not get a vote, as he or she is not technically a publicly elected member of the school board)—but was this voice representative of all of the students?

Student voice is about intentionally engaging with students on matters where they can legitimately have an influence on outcomes concerning the educational environment in which they will learn.

Furthermore, student voice is about intentionally seeking out the voices of students who are typically not heard. This includes the voices of the disengaged, the underachieving, the poor attendees, the nonparticipants, and the oppositional students. Student governments will often engage the voices of those students who value and usually flourish within the existing system. Student voice also focuses on hearing from those for whom the system is not working. When their voices can be heard and, ideally, their intellect engaged in the process of their education and the environment in which that occurs, we are most likely to create changes that will benefit a greater range of students. Such changes and the assumed engagement increases should lead to greater success for all of our students with the concomitant gains in achievement and school completion that we are seeking for our society's benefit.

SPEAK UP seeks to address the many means by which the voices of students can be heard and meaningful contributions can be made to decisions about schooling and education. The initiative consists of three key elements: student voice projects, the Minister's Student Advisory Council, and student forums. The student voice projects allow students and school staff to receive funding for a project that they feel is important to the improvement of their school from a student's perspective. While many elements of the education system in Ontario are beyond the scope of students (and often staff) to change, there are many elements of the education experience that students can influence, shape, and change. These projects assist in allowing these changes to occur and for students to become more highly engaged in their school experience by developing a real sense that their thoughts and ideas matter, and can influence and bring about positive change.

The Minister's Student Advisory Council (MSAC) is a group of sixty students who are selected for positions on a council that discusses issues of importance and who meet twice annually to provide direct feedback to the elected minister of education. Begun in 2008, this council is intended to model the importance of student input to changing the educational environment from the highest provincial level to the classroom. The group has already made suggestions that have resulted in policy changes for education in Ontario and thus demonstrates the power of the concept. The group is intended to be representative of the spectrum of students and student experiences across the province.

Student forums take various forms but are regionally focused sessions in which a larger sample of students are brought together to discuss and make suggestions on issues of interest to them. It was one such set of forums that led to the suggestions by the MSAC that resulted in policy changes to Ontario's approach to graduation requirements. For instance, the council advocated for a policy change to allow students to begin accumulating the forty hours of community involvement required for graduation in the summer between Grades 8 and 9. Previously, students had to wait until they had begun Grade 9 to start accumulating these hours. As older students often have more demands on their time, including part-time jobs, this change was considered and accepted, and the policy was changed.

Recently, the focus of the forums was adjusted slightly to encourage students to engage in action research on issues of importance to them. Some of the initial projects suggested indicate that these research-focused undertakings may provide deep insights into meaningful and relevant topics that could represent significant change opportunities for students in risk situations. These forums allow the Ministry of Education to gather student input to inform their policies and actions. At a school level, there is also a product called SPEAK UP in a Box, which allows students to run a school-wide forum following the same process and to have input on their own school's issues.

Student Choice

Choice in what we choose to study or pay attention to in life is a fundamental need for adults and students alike. The greater our options are, the more likely we are to be engaged in making those choices. Options for students must be carefully considered by school and system administrators. While much of the educational experience is determined by government policies, rules, and legislation, and further refined by local school district policies and rules, there are areas in which flexibility and options may be developed. The system in Ontario and elsewhere also has a tendency to prescribe the course and curriculum content for students in the early years of their secondary education before opening the options more broadly in Grades 11 and 12. The transitions strategy and work supervised by Dr. Bruce Ferguson, discussed earlier (Tilleczek et al., 2005, 2009), illustrate that students need flexibility to be fully engaged in their own education and subsequently to have the optimal opportunity to be successful in that education. Student choice may be ingrained in the operating processes of a school or a district (student governance structures, opportunities for students to be heard in a meaningful way, course options, and specialized program choices), but it may have the greatest impact at the classroom level. In the classroom, a teacher who is continually assessing student learning needs and differentiating the instruction to provide students with choices as to how they engage with the learning topics and materials will allow for the greatest degree of flexibility and choice for students. The work of Tomlinson (1999), Nunley (2001), and others indicates that such differentiation will result in greater success for students.

On a school level, options for students to explore areas of high interest and skill early in their secondary career will inevitably lead to greater engagement and success. An example of this is the strength-based timetable approach for students entering Grade 9, the first year of secondary school. Strength-based timetables work by using knowledge of the student's strengths to create a timetable of courses that best align with those strengths. Given the importance that Dr. Alan King's (2003, 2005) studies put on attaining all credits in the first two years of high school as an indicator of graduation success, this form of choice becomes very important. Similarly, schools in Ontario have the ability to apply for funding to support specialized programming in the senior years of secondary school: the SHSM program described earlier that offers students a chance to explore a specialized pathway toward an employment sector or sectors that engage them. Students need choices to become optimally engaged in their education, and these programs represent some of the ways in which this can be accomplished.

Student Success Teams

As described previously, the Student Success team is responsible for all aspects of the Student Success strategy and its implementation in secondary schools. These teams provide an excellent leadership focus for the strategy and are a group with whom the Ministry and SSLs can work to leverage change in secondary schools. Ideally, the teams expand to include other staff beyond the four indicated by policy, and the work of student success is internalized by all staff in the school. To a large extent, the degree to which this occurs mirrors the extent to which student risk is minimized and achievement outcomes are maximized.

The Secondary School Community Culture and Caring Strategy

How to Re-Create These Strategies

The consideration and mitigation of nonacademic barriers to success remain a challenge in all educational systems. Strong steps and gains are being made in most Ontario school districts. The following is a series of considerations for addressing these challenges, learning from the Ontario model.

Fundamental Beliefs

The underpinning principles of the community, culture, and caring strategy center on the belief that all students can learn and that the nonacademic component of readiness to learn needs to be an important area of focus. Often, the role of educators is one of facilitation to support students through the access of other services.

Key Strategies

- A clear and explicitly communicated framework for success, including fundamental beliefs and principles, intended outcomes, and supports
- The consideration of individual student situations and the subsequent identification and facilitation of appropriate supports
- Partnerships with a broader service community
- Targeted focus on students at risk of not graduating or in risk situations, and a dedication to ameliorating these issues

Political Elements

Support of education departments is helpful to align findings and to guide the development of the framework, resources, and strategies.

Reaching Teachers

The engagement of teachers and school administrators is critical in the implementation of any successful educational program. Educators must be supported with a clear vision of the intended outcome of endeavors, such as the community, culture, and caring (including transitions) strategy; and opportunity to actively apply their experience to the service of students and their families. Professional learning, resources, and communication are required to successfully implement this strategy.

Reaching School Districts

School districts need to be supported by clear communications and funding plans, training schedules, and the resources necessary to allow teachers and administrators to access the knowledge, skills training, and the tools to implement the strategies outlined here.

> **Resources and Supports**
>
> Specific transitions and support training, targeted focus sessions aimed at assisting students, and the development of professional learning teams and funding to support the objectives of the framework generated for the school or district are necessary to successfully implement this strategy.

References

Gardner, H. (1983) *Frames of mind: The theory of multiple intelligences.* New York: Basic Books.

Government of Ontario. (2003). *Building pathways for success: Final report of the Program Pathways for Students at Risk Work Group.* Toronto: Queen's Printer for Ontario.

Government of Ontario. (2010a). *Growing success: Assessment, evaluation, and reporting in Ontario schools.* Toronto: Queen's Printer for Ontario.

Government of Ontario. (2010b). *The K–12 School Effectiveness Framework: A support for school improvement and student success.* Toronto: Queen's Printer for Ontario.

King, A. J. C. (2002). *Double cohort study: Phase 2 report.* Toronto: Ontario Ministry of Education.

King, A. J. C. (2005). *Double cohort study: Phase 4 report.* Toronto: Ontario Ministry of Education.

King, A. J. C., Warren, W. K., King, M. A., Brook, J. E., & Kocher, P. R. (2009, October 20). *Who doesn't go to post-secondary education? Final report of findings.* Toronto: Colleges Ontario. Retrieved from http://www.collegesontario .org/research/who-doesnt-go-to-pse.pdf

Maslow, A. (1943). A theory of human motivation. *Psychological Review, 50*(4), 370–396.

Mourshed, M., Chijioke, C., & Barber, M. (2010). *How the world's best educations systems keep getting better.* New York: McKinsey & Company.

Nunley, K. F. (2001). *Layered curriculum: The practical solution for teachers with more than one student in their classroom.* Kearney, NH: Author.

Ontario Ministry of Education. (2003). *Think literacy success: The report of the Expert Panel on Students at Risk in Ontario.* Toronto: Expert Panel on Students at Risk in Ontario.

Ontario Ministry of Education. (2004). *Leading math success: Mathematical literacy Grades 7–12: The report of the Expert Panel on Student Success in Ontario.* Toronto: Expert Panel on Students at Risk in Ontario.

Ontario Ministry of Education. (2005, June 27). *Use of additional teacher resources to support student success in Ontario secondary schools* (Policy/Program Memorandum 137). Toronto: Government of Ontario. Retrieved from www.edu.gov.on.ca/extra/eng/ppm/137.html

Suurtamm, C., & Graves, B. (2007). *Curriculum Implementation in Mathematics (CIIM): Research Report.* Report prepared for distribution to school boards. Ottawa, Canada: University of Ottawa.

Orpwood, G., Schoolen, L., Leek, G., Marinelli-Henriques, P., & Assiri, H. (2012). *The College Math Project Final Report:* Toronto, Canada: Seneca College Applied Arts and Technology.

Tilleczek, K., Ferguson, B., Boydell, K., & Rummens, J. A. (2005). *Early school leavers: Understanding the lived reality of student disengagement from secondary school.* Toronto: Ontario Ministry of Education.

Tilleczek, K., Laflamme, S., Ferguson, B., Edney, R., Girard, M., Cudney, D., et al. (2009). *Fresh starts and false starts: Young people in transition from elementary to secondary school.* Toronto: Ontario Ministry of Education.

Tomlinson, C. (1999). *The differentiated classroom: Responding to the needs of all learners.* Alexandria, VA: Association for Supervision & Curriculum Development.

Willms, J. D., Friesen, S., & Milton, P. (2009). *What did you do in school today? Transforming classrooms through social, academic, and intellectual engagement* (First National Report). Toronto: Canadian Education Association.

6

Leadership for Improved Learning

As we contemplate the future world that our children and grand-children will inherit, one thing is clear: Their world will be increasingly diverse and complex. The knowledge and skills that they will need in twenty years will be markedly different from what school systems currently provide. In a highly complex, rapidly changing world, education will continue to be the ultimate tool of empowerment. Educational leaders have the opportunity to shape districts and schools that will provide every student with the skills and knowledge that will help them thrive in the future and lead a successful and productive life. Their influence is instrumental in creating learning environments that will help improve the life choices and chances for every child.

It is widely acknowledged that school leadership is second only to teaching in impact on student achievement (Leithwood, Louis, Anderson, & Wahlstrom, 2004; Waters, Marzano, & McNulty 2004). District leadership has also been shown to have a direct correlation to student achievement (Marzano & Waters, 2006). District and school administrators have the power to influence the day-to-day actions of staff and students. It is therefore important that they use their influence to instill a sense of moral purpose and urgency to improve educational outcomes for all students. District leaders, principals, and teacher leaders have key roles to play in achieving excellence and equity in all schools.

Leadership for the 21st Century

The world is changing rapidly, and to be able to shape that change rather than be victims of it, educational leaders need to be forward thinking visionaries who are inclusive in their leadership style. When one looks back at the industrial age, leaders tended to be autocratic and highly directive. They would tell employees what to do, often managing problems and issues on their own. We recognize that autocratic power-based leadership has become obsolete. Today, leaders know that engaging all members of the organization in improvement efforts capitalizes on the wide range of talents, knowledge, and expertise within the organization and results in "best thinking." Leaders need to use their influence to help shape the values of the organization, the behavior of those within the organization—their thinking, beliefs, and values as well as their hearts and minds—and ways of working with others. For leaders to be successful, they must be able to achieve results through the effort and support of others. They must be able to read people and the situation effectively to influence an outcome. In the past, leaders operated on the notion that their position or authority was enough to bring employees to their way of thinking and to guide their actions. Today, it is recognized that developing influencing skills is a much more effective way to bring about change.

Effective leaders in the 21st century will need to be transformational leaders that facilitate collaborative decision making and motivate everyone in the organization to take responsibility for continuous improvement. Effective leaders in education are not satisfied with the status quo; they focus on where the organization should be and create a preferred future that will ensure the success of all students. With the complexity of educational organizations, effective leaders must be flexible in their leadership style to deal effectively with the range of situations that arise. Effective leaders identify and develop a dominant style that will best serve the organization, but recognize that they may have to use differing styles when required. Table 6.1 shows a continuum of leadership styles, some of which are far more effective than others.

There may be times when a leader's manner may reflect aspects of all of these leadership styles. For example, while we know that top-down, autocratic leadership is no longer effective as the sole manner of dealing with an organization, there are times when it is essential for a principal of a school to be directive and authoritative for the safety of students or staff. A district or school leader needs to have the confidence to make a decision quickly if it means the safety or personal well-being

Table 6.1 Leadership Styles

Autocratic	• Is highly directive • Issues orders • Solves problems in isolation
Democratic	• Shares decision making
Laissez-Faire	• Believes that employees will do the right things without direction
Transactional	• Exchanges rewards for expected behavior
Transformational	• Makes decisions collaboratively • Motivates employees to work together for the good of the organization
Managerial	• Makes the operational activities of the organization the priority • Maintains the status quo
Situational	• Adapts leadership style to meet the needs of varying situations
Charismatic	• Motivates staff and inspires staff through personal attributes of the leader; has personal appeal • Draws people into a vision around a purpose • Places focus on the leader rather than the efforts of the team
Visionary	• Has a clearly defined vision of a preferred future • Establishes goals to achieve a set direction for the organization
Moral	• Is guided by what is morally right

Source: Glaze, Mattingley, & Andrews (2013).

of students. Heifetz (2006) refers to these kinds of issues as technical problems, those that have known solutions and can be handled with authoritative expertise. He goes on to point out that many of the issues facing educational leaders are adaptive challenges that require leaders to change the hearts and minds, attitudes, and behaviors of the people with whom they work. Goldberg (2001) describes five common leadership qualities that exceptional educational leaders possess. He based his observations on interviews he conducted with a wide range of educational leaders since 1989. He points out that these leaders held a bedrock belief in what they were doing. He states that they had the courage to swim upstream on behalf of their beliefs and that they possessed a social conscience to do what was morally right. They maintained a seriousness of purpose, demonstrating integrity, perseverance, and rigor, and demonstrated situational mastery that requires one to fit his or her talents and skills to goals to be achieved. In their study of how leadership influences student learning, Leithwood et al. (2004) point out that "Impressive evidence suggests that individual leaders actually behave quite differently (and productively) depending on the circumstances they are facing and the people with whom they are working" (p. 10). They stress the importance of developing leaders with a large range of leadership practices and the ability to determine the most appropriate practice for any given situation.

When looking at the overall leadership styles that are required for educational systems to achieve at high levels and help all students succeed, we need leaders who believe it is their moral responsibility to educate all students to the highest possible level. Moral leaders put the success of their students ahead of everything else. They put the best interests of their students ahead of the demands of their staff and the personal interests of the community. They are advocates first and foremost for their students. Moral leaders are not afraid to do what is right, instead of what is popular.

Leadership Development in Ontario

Like many jurisdictions, Ontario recognizes that "the progress and success of all students in the province is contingent on having effective leadership at every level to guide and support teaching and learning in Ontario schools" (Ontario Ministry of Education, 2010, p. 3). Effective leadership is essential at all levels if improvement in student achievement is to occur. There must be collaboration and communication between and within the various levels. Table 6.2 gives a broad overview of the leadership responsibilities within Ontario.

Table 6.2　Ontario Leadership Roles and Responsibilities

Provincial level	Senior ministry officials	• Develop provincial policy • Monitor implementation of ministry policy • Allocate funding and resources
District level	Directors of education	• Serve as chief executive officer for the school board • Set strategic direction of the board • Work with elected school trustees to set board policy • Ensure compliance with all ministry policies and priorities • Monitor student progress • Set budgetary priorities • Report publicly on achievement of board strategic goals

	Superintendents	• Assist the director in the development of the board strategic plan • Ensures curriculum, teaching, and learning excellence • Monitor school progress in achieving board priorities and school improvement plan goals • Liaise with community partners to achieve board goals • Ensures that schools best serve the needs of students • Conduct principal performance appraisal • Support mentorships programs for newly appointed principals and vice-principals
	School effectiveness leaders	• Are usually supervisory officers or central office administrators • Are responsible for ensuring schools conduct self-assessments • Plan and carry out district reviews for school effectiveness • Ensure school staff receive professional learning opportunities to support school self-assessment and school effectiveness • Monitor school progress in improving student achievement • Liaise with ministry staff to ensure local implementation of ministry policy and initiatives
	Student Success leaders	• Are usually supervisory officers or central office administrators • Work with high school Student Success leaders to implement strategies to improve student achievement • Ensure school staff receive professional learning opportunities to improve learning opportunities in high schools • Work with the community to extend learning opportunities and supports for high school students • Monitor student achievement in high schools
School level	Principals	• Develop school improvement plan • Monitor student progress • Monitor implementation of the Ontario Curriculum • Liaise with school parent council • Conduct principal and vice-principal and teacher performance appraisals • Mentor and train vice-principals • Communicate with the community
	Vice-principals	• Conduct teacher performance appraisals • Assist the principal in the school's administrative duties • Assist principal in the implementation and monitoring of the school improvement plan

To support and strengthen leadership in Ontario, the Ministry of Education launched the Ontario Leadership Strategy in 2008 (Ontario Ministry of Education, 2011b). The Ontario Leadership Strategy has two main goals: first, to attract the right people to the role of principal and, second, to help principals and vice-principals develop into effective instructional leaders. This initiative provides funds for boards to implement a board leadership development strategy with the central focus being improved student achievement. The foundation of the leadership strategy is the Ontario Leadership Framework. The framework identifies leadership practices that research has shown have a positive impact on student achievement. It was developed following extensive research on leadership and consultations with leaders across the province. The leadership framework outlines five domains of leadership practices and competencies. Those domains include setting directions, building relationships and developing people, developing the organization, leading the instructional program, and securing accountability. The framework also identifies five core leadership capacities that effective leaders demonstrate:

- Setting goals
- Aligning resources with priorities
- Promoting collaborative learning cultures
- Using data
- Engaging in courageous conversations

In 2009–2010, the Ministry made the five core leadership competencies a focus for all provincially sponsored professional learning (Ontario Ministry of Education, 2009a).

The leadership framework consists of two parts: Part 1 examines leadership practices and competencies, and Part 2 looks at system practices and procedures (see Institute for Education Leadership, 2012). The leadership framework provides a basis for discussion on the characteristics of effective leadership. Ontario's educational leaders are encouraged to use the framework as a tool for self-reflection and personal growth. Districts across the province have used it as a foundation for leadership development. Districts have also used the framework to conduct a gap analysis regarding district leadership to determine which practices and competencies are currently in place and which ones need further development.

Performance appraisal also plays a large role in leadership development. In consultation with principals, the Ministry developed a principal performance appraisal system that provides opportunities for formal feedback based on the competencies identified in the Ontario Leadership Framework (Ontario Ministry of Education, 2009b). Superintendents in Ontario are responsible for conducting principal performance appraisals, with principals being responsible for conducting appraisals of vice-principals. The performance appraisal process gives school administrators the opportunity to reflect on their strengths and areas in need of improvement, engage in a dialogue about their performance with their supervisor, and discuss supports needed to achieve their goals for professional growth. Principals and vice-principals are appraised on their progress in achieving goals identified in their school improvement plans and effectiveness in demonstrating the leadership framework competencies. Each school administrator is required to develop a performance plan in consultation with the appraiser based on the school improvement plan, the district's strategic goals, and ministry priorities. To assist school administrators in achieving goals outlined in their performance plan, they are expected to develop an annual growth plan that outlines strategies for growth and development based on the practices and competencies identified in the Ontario Leadership Framework.

To support newly appointed principals and supervisory officers (directors and superintendents), the Ministry implemented mentorship programs. All school districts receive funding as part of the Board Leadership Development Strategy and are required to provide mentoring to all newly appointed principals and vice-principals for their first two years in the role. In the manual *Mentoring for Newly Appointed School Leaders* (Ontario Ministry of Education, 2011a), the Ministry outlines mentoring expectations for districts.

In addition, the Ministry also supports mentoring programs for supervisory officers. The program matches senior administrators new to the role with experienced supervisory officers. The mentors assist mentees in reflecting on their practice in light of the competencies outlined in the leadership framework, reviewing current issues and in problem solving. Mentors and mentees engage in face-to-face meetings a set number of times during the year and have ongoing contact via e-mail and telephone conversations. Mentors regularly review with the mentee their learning plan, progress in achieving goals and next steps. Mentorship relationships are generally one year in duration, with the option for a second year if requested by the mentee.

The Ministry of Education also established the Institute for Education Leadership in partnership with Ontario's principals' councils and supervisory officer organizations. The institute supports Ontario's educational leaders by providing ongoing professional development and resources, as well as conducting research into the leadership practices that have a positive impact on student achievement. The institute also developed the "Leadership Self-Review Tool" to help boards in assessing their effectiveness in supporting leadership practices within their schools.

In 2010–2011, the Ministry required all district school boards to establish a board leadership development strategy and to appoint a leader and steering committee to guide the implementation, monitoring, and evaluation of the strategy. They were also expected to appoint a lead person (or leads) for mentoring newly appointed school leaders and for the process of principal/vice-principal performance appraisal. The Ministry supported the work of the boards through direct funding to the board and through provision of resources and professional learning opportunities. By supporting boards in the creation of a leadership development strategy, the Ministry has ensured consistency in leadership development, while at the same time allowing flexibility to meet local needs. Ontario believes that strengthening district and school leadership is vital to improving student achievement and graduation rates.

Professional Learning Opportunities

The Ministry of Education recognized from the onset of its improvement strategy that there was a great deal of expertise to be tapped across the province. Professional learning opportunities were provided that enabled educational leaders at various levels to discuss current issues and challenges, share promising practices, and link with colleagues in similar circumstances. Provincial conferences, regional meetings, webcasts, print resources, and funding for leadership development were just a few of the ongoing supports the province provided to support leaders in improvement efforts. The Literacy and Numeracy Secretariat provided opportunities for directors of education from high-achieving school districts and low-achieving school districts to come together through what was at the time called the Leadership Alliance Network for Student Achievement (LANSA). These directors were invited to come together to discuss barriers to improved student achievement and to develop solutions to support improvement.

In partnership with Ontario principals' associations, the Secretariat launched Leading Student Achievement networks for learning. This initiative provides professional learning and networking opportunities across districts with the goal of improving instructional leadership. The project began in 2005 with a handful of elementary school principals from across the province. Today, the initiative has elementary school principals involved from 54 districts in the province as well as secondary school principals from 26 districts. The program has grown steadily since its inception in 2005. This is a testament to the value that principals see in working together with other principals from across the province to improve achievement in their schools.

The Leading Student Achievement (LSA) project provides the opportunity for principals from various locations across the province to work in teams to strengthen instructional leadership. The project is designed around a tri-level model: school, district, and province. This means that principals work within their own schools to improve instructional practice and the conditions that improve student learning. They then share their experience, successes, challenges, and key learnings with their principal learning teams, which include principals from other districts. There is also support from the provincial level through the Leading Student Achievement steering team, which provides support through a variety of professional learning opportunities and resources. Principals in the project focus on collaborative inquiry processes and the school conditions that have the greatest impact on student learning.

The Ministry of Education is committed to research and increasing the knowledge base regarding effective leadership. To that end, Leithwood was invited to work with the Leading Student Achievement project to evaluate the impact of the project. His paper "How the *Leading Student Achievement* Project Improves Student Learning: An Evolving Theory of Action" (2010) outlines the impact of such an approach. He points out that since its inception, the Leading Student Achievement initiative has become more precise in its work and is focusing on key areas that research has shown have a positive impact on student achievement.

Succession Planning

The true sign of good leaders is the number of great leaders they leave in their wake. If reform measures are to be sustained, it is vital for jurisdictions to develop well-thought-out succession plans. That is why Ontario has made succession planning one aspect of its leadership strategy. Like many jurisdictions, Ontario realized that many of its principals would be retiring in a relatively short time. The Ontario Principal's Council conducted a study in 2001 that showed that by 2009, more than 80% of Ontario's elementary and secondary principals would be eligible to retire (Ontario Ministry of Education, 2008). It was, therefore, essential that Ontario step up its efforts for leadership development and encourage boards to establish succession plans to address the situation. Ontario is not alone in its need to recruit and train future leaders. Many jurisdictions around the globe have an aging group of school and district administrators that will be retiring in the near future. The Ministry of Education has identified successful practices for succession planning. They support mentoring, coaching, and induction programs for newly appointed administrators and encourage boards to institute leadership development programs. It is important for succession planning to identify recruitment strategies that will appoint leadership candidates from diverse populations that reflect the diversity of the jurisdiction. Students need to see their cultures reflected in the leadership of their schools.

In a report commissioned by the Institute for Education Leadership (2008), a number of promising practices for succession planning were identified. Those included

- early identification of leadership candidates,
- mentoring and coaching of potential candidates and newly appointed leaders,
- providing leadership courses and workshops,
- opportunities for hands-on practical experiences,
- providing networking opportunities,
- equitable recruitment processes, and
- ongoing support and professional learning for current leaders.

Jurisdictions might want to consider the following questions when developing their succession plan:

- How many leadership positions will we need to fill five years from now? Ten years from now?
- How are we communicating the organization's leadership needs to our employees?
- How will we know that we have established an effective leadership development program?
- How do we identify and support future leaders?
- Do we have a recruitment process that ensures equity?
- Does our leadership group reflect the diversity of the district's population?
- What resources are required to implement our succession plan?
- How do we support professional learning and leadership development?
- What competencies will be required of future leaders in the organization?
- How do we ensure that all employees are aware of leadership opportunities?
- How do we assist staff with personal career planning?

Planning for the turnover in leadership positions ensures that the best possible candidates are recruited. The success of any educational organization is dependent on the recruitment and retention of high quality leaders through a well-thought-out succession plan—a plan that is proactive in identifying trends and future leadership needs. If we are to improve student outcomes, we must ensure that we have high-quality leaders in our schools and districts.

Effective Leadership: What Does It Take?

Many believe that successful leaders are charismatic, but it doesn't stop there. The focus cannot just be on them; it must be on developing an effective team and a collaborative culture. They facilitate shared leadership and build on the strengths of those in the organization. Fullan (2001) goes so far as to say that "charismatic leaders inadvertently often do more harm than good because, at best, they provide episodic improvement followed by frustrated or despondent dependency" (p. 1). He stresses that deep and sustained reform depends on many people, not just the extraordinary leader. If leaders are solely dependent on charisma, rather than the other leadership characteristics we have described, they rarely build a sense of shared leadership. The danger rests in the fact that when the leader leaves, the vision often leaves as well. Effective leaders use their influence to shape attitudes, develop leaders, and instill a sense of responsibility and ownership for the future vision of the organization. As Hargreaves and Fink (2003) also stress, to sustain the changes that leaders initiate, leadership must be embedded in the "hearts and minds of the many and not rest on the shoulders of the heroic few" (p. 699).

Effective leaders practice transformational leadership. They build on the talents and strengths of their colleagues in the organization. They develop a collaborative culture that encourages shared leadership. They encourage and support those in the organization to work together to achieve improvement goals.

District and school administrators who have been successful in improving student learning are agents of hope. They hold a clear vision of a preferred future, where educators hold high expectations for all students and accept responsibility for the success of every student. They are committed to their moral responsibility to make a difference in the lives of every child and educate all children to the highest possible level. They are committed not only to excellence but also to equity of outcomes. They are as concerned as much about the school down the street as their own school. Their goal is to see all students in their district succeed. Morally driven leaders instill a sense of urgency in those around them to achieve continuous improvement in educational outcomes. They drive home the message that the children cannot wait, and that we must close gaps in achievement and improve the life choices and chances of all children.

For educational leaders to be successful in the 21st century, they will need to

- focus on excellence and equity,
- develop future leaders,
- influence others,
- be instructional leaders,
- be strategic managers,
- facilitate shared leadership,
- build relationships,
- be courageous,
- be strategic,
- be politically astute,
- inspire public confidence, and
- achieve results.

Strategic Managers

Effective leaders are not just managers. They are not guardians of the status quo, and they don't look at the operational side of the organization as the priority. That being said, effective leaders cannot ignore the day-to-day operations. By strategically managing the operations of the district and schools, educational leaders can ensure that resources are effectively deployed to meet improvement goals. District and school leaders need to make the tough decisions on how to allocate limited resources. Treating students equitably does not necessarily mean treating them the same. It may mean providing additional funds to schools in challenging circumstances or to specific programs for students who are underperforming. It means disaggregating data to determine the schools and groups of students who are struggling, and then strategically allocating the supports needed to improve outcomes. It is also essential that district and school leaders ensure that staffing decisions reflect the needs of students and the diversity of the school population. Educational leaders that are strategic managers are intentional in their hiring. One of the most important tasks that superintendents and principals are charged with is hiring the best people, assigning staff, and promoting them. It is critical that they realize that the most successful intervention for students who are struggling is to ensure that they have the highest-quality teachers. Unfortunately, it is not uncommon for our least-experienced teachers to be assigned to schools where children live in poverty, or to schools with large numbers of students of visible minorities (Barton, 2003). Superintendents and principals are wise to put their most qualified and highly skilled people and resources into the schools and classes that need them most. District and school leaders need to reach out to the outstanding educators they know and invite them and persuade them to transfer to where they are needed most. In addition, every effort should be made to have staff members who reflect the backgrounds of the community. Students feel more connected to their school when they see their own culture and background reflected in the school environment. Educational leaders should work collaboratively with teacher unions to review and revise in-school assignments and transfer practices so that schools can be served more equitably. By ensuring that our most needy students get our best teachers, we can improve graduation rates.

Strategic managers ensure that organizational structures are in place that will facilitate high-quality instruction. They work with staff to design timetables that enhance learning. For example, they develop expectations for uninterrupted blocks of time for literacy and numeracy instruction in elementary schools. They ensure that instructional time is not compromised by frequent interruptions or distractions. The old notion of time on task remains a research-informed strategy. They allocate resources that support teachers in meeting school improvement goals. Horng and Loeb (2010) stress that schools that demonstrate improved student achievement are more likely to have principals who are strong organizational managers. Being a strategic manager is one of many leadership qualities that can improve student outcomes.

Shared Leadership

Outstanding leaders recognize that in the complex world we face, everyone's intelligence is needed; therefore, they develop a culture of shared leadership and engage everyone in improvement efforts. They encourage participation in district and school-wide decision making. Shared leadership results in people feeling valued and engaged so that they take ownership and shared responsibility for finding solutions to challenges the district or school might face. Leaders who develop a culture of shared leadership capitalize on the expertise, talent, and knowledge of the group. They establish a climate of trust and respect, empowering those with whom they work to step forward and share their ideas. They build relationships that foster confidence and a sense of worth among their staff. In a culture of shared leadership, knowledge and practice get stretched across roles rather than being inherent in one role or another. Wahlstrom, Louis, Leithwood, and Anderson (2010) found that when teachers and principals shared leadership, teachers' working relationships are stronger, and student achievement is higher.

Building Relationships

Effective leaders know the importance of building relationships. They need to recognize that everyone in the organization is at a different place, and they need to bring them forward from that place. They need to build a climate of trust and respect where educators feel safe to try new strategies to improve student achievement in an environment that is nonpunitive for risk takers. Building an environment where educators work collaboratively and challenge one another in a respectful and professional manner is essential for administrators who lead their organizations to new heights of attainment.

While we don't like to think that politics enters into educational leadership, the reality is that whenever you are dealing with human relationships, there are political overtones. Whether it be the parent council, the school board, or local or state (provincial) politicians, politics will affect the dynamics of the organization and ultimately the decisions regarding the education of our children. Effective leaders need to be politically astute. They need to understand the issues and how they can impact the organization. Building partnerships and relationships with the groups that have a stake in public education can be very beneficial. By forming relationships, leaders better understand the issues and priorities of various groups and diverse viewpoints. Investing time in forming relationships and providing open and honest communication can help avoid misunderstandings, bring diverse groups on board, and make for better decision making. By sharing district and school goals and actions, leaders can build support for the organization. Heifetz and Linsky (2004) suggest that leaders should keep the opposition close and work as closely with opponents as one would supporters. They suggest that is crucial for leaders to understand one's opponent's perspectives and address those issues as you move forward. Political acuity is an essential skill for effective leaders.

Instructional Leadership

We need district and school leaders who are instructional leaders with a relentless focus on student learning and achievement. They need to mobilize resources to create 21st century schools where excellence and equity go hand in hand.

One of the biggest problems with improvement efforts is that, often, not everyone in the organization buys in. If the improvement agenda is not owned by everyone, you get spotty implementation and improvement efforts are not effective. Instructional leaders must push for consistent implementation of the research-informed strategies that have been shown to positively affect student achievement. Effective instructional leaders provide pressure and targeted support to achieve consistency across classrooms.

Instructional leaders are lead learners who focus on student learning. They are relentless in achieving equity of outcomes and are committed to continuous improvement. Instructional leaders are instrumental in developing effective professional learning communities and a collaborative culture. They are knowledgeable about curriculum and instruction and are consumers of current research into best practice. They are not afraid to show their staff that they don't have all the answers or are experts on everything, but are committed to learning alongside their staff. District and school leaders who are instructional leaders set high expectations for themselves and all staff. They monitor classroom practice and provide support and coaching to others. They are committed to the use of data to inform improvement planning and classroom instruction and to monitor student achievement. Instructional leaders have the courage to stand up for what they know is right, to ensure that all students have access to the instructional strategies that we know work.

Courageous Leadership

To bring about change, leaders must be willing to question the status quo; they must be courageous and be willing to take risks. They have to be willing to ask the tough questions. Courageous district and school leaders put students first and are not afraid to initiate change. They identify problems and develop a climate of trust and respect, and encourage those in the organization to raise issues and concerns. They are open and transparent about the challenges the organization faces and the steps to be taken for improvement. Courageous leaders have a high tolerance for the truth. They seek input from staff and the community and encourage open and honest dialogue. Courageous leaders disaggregate achievement data to determine the groups of students who are not achieving and engage everyone in identifying strategies to give those students a hand up and to close achievement gaps. Courageous leaders are not afraid to admit to mistakes and to learn from them. They work with colleagues to develop new approaches when the status quo is not working.

Many people will avoid courageous conversations because they can be uncomfortable and create conflict. Without these conversations, however, change won't happen. Districts and schools will not be able to get to the root of inequities and overcome them. District and school leaders need to be prepared to have tough conversations when they see that district and school practices and policies are not improving student achievement. They must accept responsibility and take the necessary actions to improve student outcomes. They need to speak out publicly and be advocates for the success of all students. They need to be solution finders.

District Leadership

Achieving and sustaining systemic change requires a district vision, consistency in direction, and action over an extended period. District leaders play a critical role in establishing a culture of high expectations. They need to be open about what is working within the district and what is not. If students in their districts are not achieving at acceptable levels, they have to be willing to shake things up and challenge the status quo. District leaders need to develop a shared vision and awaken in all educators in their district a sense of moral purpose to educate all students to the highest possible level. They may need to initiate organizational changes in staff responsibilities and revise policies to ensure improvement goals are achieved. District leaders must regularly monitor the progress of all students, disaggregating data to determine the groups of students who are underachieving. They are charged with guiding budget deliberations and the allocation of resources to ensure that improvement strategies are properly resourced and that those schools that are struggling get the additional supports they require to succeed. One example of shifting resources is to recognize that schools in challenging circumstances may need smaller class sizes in the early grades and differentiated staffing to meet unique needs. Policy makers and educational leaders have the ability to question current practices that do not result in equitable outcomes for students and make the changes necessary that ensure that students from challenging circumstances don't end up in schools with fewer resources.

Strategies for District Leaders

- Establish a clear vision for the district and a small number of well articulated goals.
- Establish high expectations for all students.
- Focus on equity and excellence.
- Make professional learning a priority in the district.
- Visit schools regularly to monitor progress in achieving district student learning goals.
- Recruit, develop, and support the best people possible for leadership positions.
- Align resources with district priorities.
- Use data effectively to inform decision making.
- Focus on continuous improvement.
- Develop partnerships to support student success.
- Focus on results for students in general and those in challenging circumstances in particular.

School Leadership

Research has shown that effective principal and vice-principal leadership can positively impact student achievement. Wahlstrom et al. (2010) have shown through their research that "the effects of school leadership directly influence school and classroom conditions, as well as teachers themselves, and indirectly influence student learning" (p. 5). Principals have the ability to influence the day-to-day actions of their staff. Through their actions, they can create the conditions necessary to improve instruction for all students. Effective school leadership is a strong catalyst for improving student outcomes and closing gaps in student achievement. It is important that they use their influence to instill a sense of urgency within their schools to improve achievement for the students who are struggling, and to put in place the systems and processes that will lead to better results.

Leadership is about learning. Principals and teachers should work together to learn about current research in effective instructional practice. Effective principals learn along with the staff and encourage shared decision making and group thinking.

Strategies for Principals

- Keep school improvement goals and strategies at the forefront. Review school goals at staff meetings and progress being made in the implementation of the strategies to achieve goals. Ask staff to bring student work and other evidence to staff meetings to demonstrate progress in achieving the school's improvement goals.
- Build a collaborative culture where staff work together on improvement strategies and school-wide decision making.
- Encourage dialogue with staff about what's working, what's not, and how to overcome challenges.
- Assist staff in gathering evidence of effective practice and facilitate the sharing of promising practices.
- Visit classrooms regularly to monitor implementation and provide support.
- Encourage shared leadership. When teachers are empowered, they turn their schools into learning organizations where everyone becomes responsible for learning. Make school improvement a whole-school responsibility, where staff take ownership for developing improvement strategies, monitoring progress, and revising improvement plans as needed.
- Gather data regularly to monitor progress.
- Provide the necessary resources and supports for the implementation of improvement strategies.
- Communicate progress in achieving.
- Focus on results.
- Celebrate successes.
- Help others accept the fact that schools control the conditions for student success.

Teacher Leadership

Teachers possess a wealth of knowledge and expertise that benefit not only their own classroom but also the school as a whole. When district and school leaders encourage teachers to take on leadership roles, they create an environment where teachers feel included and valued. When teachers are included in district- and school-based improvement discussions, they take ownership for the implementation of improvement strategies. Teacher leadership can be both formal and informal. Formal teacher leaders may take on the role of department head, chair of a committee, coach of team, advisor to a student club, or mentor to a new colleague. Informal leadership opportunities also abound.

Teachers can gain leadership experience by coaching a colleague, leading a book study, sharing a successful practice at a staff meeting, assisting the principal with a staff meeting agenda, or organizing a special event at the school. Teacher leaders have a great deal to offer and, if nurtured and encouraged, will consider taking on roles of added responsibility. Principals should provide opportunities for teachers to take on leadership roles within the school and district, and teachers should take advantage of those opportunities to help their school achieve improvement goals. Effective leaders mentor those who will replace them.

Recognizing the talent and strengths within the staff and providing them with leadership opportunities builds staff motivation, confidence, and commitment to improvement. District and schools will benefit greatly when they take advantage of the teacher talent pool and engage them in leadership activities.

Strategies for Teachers

- Regularly reflect on current practice to determine what's working and what's not.
- Monitor student success and take pride in the impact of instructional practice when student achievement improves.
- Accept professional accountability for the success of all students.
- Be an active part of staff discussions to monitor school-wide progress.
- Collaborate with colleagues and support one another, learning with and from colleagues.
- Attend professional learning opportunities that strengthen knowledge.
- Take part in school improvement planning.
- Share promising practices with colleagues.
- Work with the principal and others to monitor success. Use school and classroom data to track progress.
- Take advantage of leadership opportunities within the district and school.
- Engage parents in meaningful ways to support improved student achievement.
- Recognize the impact of effective teaching on student success.

Summary

To improve student outcomes and increase graduation rates, we need to strengthen leadership at all levels. Research demonstrates a correlation between student achievement and the strong leadership at the district and school levels. District leaders, principals, and teacher leaders have key roles to play in developing equitable and inclusive schools—schools that have high expectations for all students and that provide the supports necessary to ensure the success of all students.

Leadership is not about having all the answers. It's about being willing to ask the right questions. It's about capitalizing on the strengths of those around you and building a team of leaders. It's about doing what is right for students. Effective leaders lead with their heart and their mind. They are advocates for every student and put student learning and success ahead of all else. Effective leaders challenge the status quo and ensure that excellence and equity go hand in hand.

References

Barton, P. (2003). *Parsing the achievement gap: Baselines for tracking progress.* Princeton, NJ: Educational Testing Service.

Fullan, M. (2001). *Leading in a culture of change.* San Francisco: Jossey-Bass.

Goldberg, M. (2001, June). Leadership in education: Five commonalities. *Phi Delta Kappan, 82*(10), 757–761.

Hargreaves, A., & Fink, D. (2003, May). Sustaining leadership. *Phi Delta Kappan, 84*(9), 693–700.

Heifetz, R. (2006, March). Educational leadership: Beyond a focus on instruction. *Phi Delta Kappan, 87*(7), 512–513.

Heifetz, R., & Linsky, M. (2004, April). When leadership spells danger. *Educational Leadership, 61*(7), 33–37.

Horng, E., & Loeb, S. (2010, November). New thinking about instructional leadership. *Phi Delta Kappan, 92*(3), 66–69.

Institute for Education Leadership. (2008, August). *Putting Ontario's leadership framework into action: A guide for school and system leaders.* Toronto, ON: Author. Retrieved from http://iel.immix.ca/storage/2/1284580690/Frame workAction.pdf

Institute for Education Leadership. (2012, August). *The Ontario Leadership Framework 2012: A school system leader's guide to putting Ontario's leadership framework into action.* Toronto, ON: Author. Retrieved from http:// iel.immix.ca/storage/6/1357935981/Ontario_Leadership_Framework .pdf

Leithwood, K. (2010). How the *Leading Student Achievement* project improves student learning: An evolving theory of action. *Curriculum Services Canada.* Retrieved from http://resources.curriculum.org/LSA/files/ LSATheoryofAction.pdf

Leithwood, K., Louis, K. S., Anderson, S., & Wahlstrom, K. (2004, September).

How leadership influences student learning: A review of research. New York: The Wallace Foundation, Center for Applied Research and Educational Improvement and Ontario Institute for Studies in Education.

Marzano, R., & Waters, J. T. (2006, September). *School district leadership that works: The effect of superintendent leadership on student achievement*. Denver, CO: Mid-continent Research for Education and Learning.

Ontario Ministry of Education. (2008). *Succession planning for Ontario schools and school boards*. Toronto, ON: Author. Retrieved from http://www .education-leadership-ontario.ca/storage/2/1284604393/Succession PlanningSummary.pdf

Ontario Ministry of Education. (2009a, Fall). Five core capacities of effective leaders. *Ideas Into Action, 1.* Retrieved from http://www.edu.gov.on.ca/ eng/policyfunding/leadership/IdeasIntoAction09.pdf

Ontario Ministry of Education. (2009b, August). *Principal/vice principal performance appraisal: Guideline for board implementation Version 3*. Toronto: Author. Retrieved from http://www.cpco.on.ca/resourcelibrary/mpa/ ppa_guideline.pdf

Ontario Ministry of Education. (2012). *Board leadership development strategy: Requirements manual*. Toronto, ON: Author. Retrieved from http://www .edu.gov.on.ca/eng/policyfunding/leadership/BLDS2012Manual.pdf

Ontario Ministry of Education. (2011a). *Ontario Leadership Strategy: Mentoring for newly appointed school leaders: Requirements manual*. Toronto, ON: Author. Retrieved from http://www.edu.gov.on.ca/eng/policyfunding/ leadership/pdfs/2011Mentoring.pdf

Ontario Ministry of Education. (2011b, June). *Ontario Leadership Strategy: Quick facts 2011–2012*. Toronto, ON: Author. Retrieved from http:// www.edu.gov.on.ca/eng/policyfunding/leadership/OLS_QuickFacts .pdf

Wahlstrom, K., Louis, K. S., Leithwood, K., & Anderson, S. (2010). *Investigating the links to improved student learning: Executive summary*. New York: The Wallace Foundation/Center for Applied Research and Educational Improvement, University of Minnesota/Ontario Institute for Studies in Education.

Waters, T., Marzano, R., & McNulty, B. (2004, April). Leadership that sparks learning. *Educational Leadership, 61*(7), 48–51.

7

Improving Graduation Rates

What Does It Take?

One of the most common observations made by educators in Ontario is that the actions taken and the strategies that were used to improve the system also helped to change the culture of schools irrevocably. Once there was deep cultural change, the common refrain was that, as professionals, they could not go back to where they were before the improvements took hold. As stated in Chapter 1, there were other changes: philosophies, mind-sets, practices, outlook, motivation, and a sense of self-efficacy. Many moved from a focus on families being responsible for student success to one that indicated schools have significant control over student outcomes. Teachers and principals began to believe that instructional effectiveness and leadership quality play an important role in school improvement and that select research-informed, high-impact strategies had a pivotal role in improving learning. More importantly, having high expectations for learning was now the norm.

This chapter provides a summary of the key processes used and discusses a few of the other conditions that supported the approach. The contribution that building community alliances to support learning made and the importance of implementing a system-wide and systematic approach to character development are also discussed as key supporting conditions.

The Essence of the Improvement Strategy

In reviewing the process we used for system change and improvement in Ontario schools, it is important to point out that the strategies worked in combination. The focus was on bringing about improvement at all levels of the system: the Ministry of Education, school districts, schools, and classrooms. The alignment of goals, strategies, intentions, and focus that was sought at these levels is an important reason for the success of the strategy. These processes included

- establishing a "guiding coalition," including the premier of Ontario and the minister of education, to support change and to monitor improvement;
- appointing as chief student achievement officer, a respected educator with experience at all levels of the system to champion the initiative;
- communicating the need for high standards and expectations;
- engaging system partners and creating the alliances necessary for improvement;
- adopting an inclusive approach and creating an important role for teacher unions and principal councils in the improvement process;
- involving other partners, such as faculties of education, to prepare research monographs to develop a strong orientation to research;
- ensuring ongoing dialogue and engagement with all stakeholders;
- forging consensus;
- developing a common sense of purpose;
- building commitment and motivation;
- selecting a small number of ambitious goals;
- supporting and guiding school improvement planning and the development of SMART goals;
- insisting on a focus on both excellence and equity and on closing achievement gaps;
- facilitating capacity building at all levels, with an emphasis on instructional effectiveness;
- investing in leadership development;
- providing positive pressure and targeted support;
- implementing research-informed, high-impact strategies to improve achievement;
- using data-informed decision making and a variety of assessment tools to improve practice;

- developing a "Statistical Neighbours" tool to validate the efforts of schools in challenging circumstances and to remove excuses for low performance;
- ensuring deep implementation and monitoring processes;
- providing targeted resources;
- promoting teacher collaboration and action research;
- conducting assessments of district and school effectiveness;
- using nonpunitive intervention strategies to improve low-performing schools;
- paying attention to the potential distractors;
- settling collective agreements;
- reducing and circumventing bureaucracy to protect the focus on the core priorities;
- supporting community outreach and engagement strategies;
- embedding opportunities for student leadership, voice, and choice;
- involving parents and community in meaningful ways;
- emphasizing the importance of professional accountability; and
- encouraging international comparability.

Reasons for the Success of the Strategy

As practitioners, we are often asked to identify the key reasons our strategy was successful in improving not only student achievement and graduation rates, but also instructional and leadership effectiveness, and teachers' sense of self-efficacy and morale at that time. Knowing what we now know about school improvement, and the strategies used by high-performing systems, we can identify a few keys to success in bringing about lasting system improvement:

- Fostering a spirit of mutual trust and collegiality
- Developing a culture of high expectations for students and professionals alike
- Rejecting the shame-and-blame or one-size-fits-all approach to school improvement
- Establishing a few precise goals and ambitious targets
- Differentiating and targeting supports to meet unique needs
- Investing in people through capacity building at all levels of the system
- Using research- and data-informed decision-making strategies

- Monitoring progress and providing early and ongoing interventions and effective feedback
- Encouraging networks and professional learning communities
- Providing coaching and mentorship for both adults and students
- Sharing successful practices and approaches
- Recognizing and celebrating success

Working at Getting Buy-In Was Important

The Ontario improvement strategy taught us that long-term improvement is made possible when a system demonstrates respect for the professionalism of teachers; eschews the shame-and-blame, one-size-fits-all approaches to system improvement; and focuses on capacity building. The truth is that if people knew what to do, they would have done it! If improvement is not being made, it means that people need to be assisted in identifying what needs to be done and developing the capacity to do it.

Undoubtedly, many factors contributed to the success of the strategy. This includes the time spent on securing buy-in from the people who were responsible for implementing the practices and innovations that would bring about success in the schools and classrooms. In other words, the focus had to be "where the rubber hits the road." Having the implementers on board was both wise and essential.

It must be made clear that there was also a need to bring about change with a sense of urgency. Too often, the idea that working at achieving buy-in requires a lot of time and should not be a focus is simply unfounded. For us, this was not the case. We worked expeditiously and were able to bring key stakeholders on board and keep them involved in providing regular input on key directions. There was also fidelity to the notion that there should be no surprises in working with partners.

Developing Partnership and Alliances With Parents and Community

The commonly used African saying "It takes a whole village to raise a child" reflects the importance of partnership development to support learning. We recognized the need to build a coalition of all partners—parents, community organizations, social agencies, business and unions, and religious, cultural, and athletic groups—to create the links necessary to facilitate student success. The fact is that schools cannot achieve success alone. Partnerships facilitate success and sustainability.

Drucker (1999), in his article "The New Pluralism," paints a picture of the expansive role that leaders play within communities and in society at large. He emphasizes the need for leaders to take care of the common good by leading beyond the walls of their institutions. In fact, he states that leaders will have to learn to create community. He exhorts educators to use the capital they have to build the communities they all wish to inhabit and leave for their children and grandchildren.

One of the conversations that is necessary today is the role of schools in society and whether or not schools can live up to the many expectations that society now has of that role. These expanded expectations and responsibilities must be shared among all community partners. The need to create the alliances necessary to support learning is one that must be embraced if student needs are to be met.

To foster the healthy development of students, it is also necessary for schools to bring together the human, financial, and material resources that exist within the community. This would allow educators to focus on the academic needs of students as their primary purpose. As a long-term strategy, this idea does resonate with educators, but with dwindling resources, optimism can sometimes be in short supply. But even in these times of challenge and uncertainty, we are convinced that it is still necessary to find new ways for people and groups to come together and combine their expertise and resources for the purpose of raising children and creating a new sense of community.

The authors support strongly the notion proposed by Sergiovanni (1994) when he said that community building must become the heart of any school improvement efforts. For him, regardless of what we are currently engaged in to support reform efforts—whether related to governance, structures, curriculum, assessment, or teacher or parent empowerment—these must all rest on a foundation of community building. More than ever, it is necessary for schools to expand their mandate well beyond their traditional educational domain to support parents in their efforts and to provide the social, emotional, physical, and other needs of children and youth today.

Raising children is a community partnership endeavor. It requires many groups and individuals to ensure that students are engaged in their learning and are successful in their educational and career pursuits. Developing school–community partnerships has many benefits to school programs, climate, and services for families. It has the potential to increase parents' skills and leadership, connect families with others in the school and in the community, and help teachers with their work (Epstein, 2001). Most importantly, school–community partnerships can help students become even more engaged in their studies and achieve the standards set out by policy makers, parents, community members, and teachers.

There are many challenges inherent in developing partnerships, especially those between schools and communities. Tensions often exist because these are two very different communities trying to work together (Israel, Schulz, Parker, & Becker, 1998). Nonetheless, the benefit of engaging in partnerships outweighs the tensions including those related to building capacity, improving efficacy, and improving outcomes (Edelstein, in press; Lasker & Weiss, 2003). Three of the most prominent characteristics that affect the development of collaborative partnerships stemming from the literature are those related to leadership, trust, and communication.

The challenges in building a relationship between the school and community lie in addressing the needs of both. Educators need to be able at all times to teach the students the curriculum, but teachers are also often mentors to their students and role models of how to behave and conduct oneself in a social forum. Some parents may not be available at all times to respond to student challenges in a timely manner due to work responsibilities or other circumstances. Teachers and principals need to be able to work with parents and the community to address the needs of students, given any external challenges. Likewise, the community body needs to be responsive to both the school and its own cultural priorities as they arise (Epstein, 2001).

Epstein's (2001) framework of six types of involvement and sample practices has been used extensively in parent and community development initiatives. She identifies the major involvements of parents as those of parenting, communicating, volunteering, learning at home, decision making, and collaborating with the community. Each of these is broken up into specific tasks that support the major priorities. All the activities that parents engage in are seen as important—whether inside or outside of the home, political or nonpolitical. Whatever parents are able to do can help to support their role in partnering with schools to support student learning and well-being.

Ross's 1994 survey of research indicates that many benefits accrue when parents are involved in their children's education. These include

- better long-term academic achievement,
- higher marks,
- higher test scores,
- higher motivation,

- more positive attitudes,
- increased commitment to schooling,
- fewer students retained in a grade,
- decreased placement in special education,
- fewer behavioral problems,
- improved average daily attendance,
- fewer school dropouts,
- lower suspension rates,
- more successful programs, and
- more effective schools.

Throughout our implementation process, we were mindful of the research on the importance of parental engagement. Involving parents was an important aspect of the strategy—one that contributed to the improvement of the system.

The Ontario Ministry of Education's parent engagement policy is outlined in *Parents in Partnership: A Parent Engagement Policy for Ontario Schools* (2010). Parent engagement is also an essential component of Ontario's equity and inclusive education strategy, which formally recognizes and supports the vision of Ontario schools as places of partnership and inclusion, where all students, parents, and other members of the school community are welcomed and respected.

The policy outlines the vision for parent involvement and recommends strategies to support parent engagement. It includes an action plan for schools, boards, and the ministry, and showcases some of the many exemplary practices that are being employed across the province. The policy includes new directions to help ensure that all partners have the skills, knowledge, and tools they need to build positive partnerships in support of student success.

Many teachers already pay special attention to the engagement of parents. In particular, teachers of children in kindergarten programs spend much time getting to know parents before students begin school. In some school districts, these programs take many forms because of the belief that it is necessary to gather information from a variety of sources to plan effective programs for students. As well, the focus on holistic education—bringing together the demographic information that can influence the academic, social, and emotional well-being of students—helps to paint a picture of their needs and the supports that are necessary from all partners in the educational process.

All administrators are encouraged to ensure that community outreach and engagement is an important component of their entry plan when they assume new assignments in school districts. It must also be an ongoing aspect of strategic direction setting if school systems intend to adopt an inclusive approach to educating children and youth. Special attention needs to be paid to the demographic makeup of communities to address unique cultural, religious, and other needs. As well, school leaders today are well advised to live up to the spirit of human rights codes and to model for students what values are inherent in living in diverse and inclusive contexts.

The *Ontario Schools, Kindergarten to Grade 12* document (Ontario Ministry of Education, 2011) states that Ontario Regulation 612/00 also mandates school boards to establish school councils and parent involvement committees (PICs) to engage parents and benefit from their advice at the school and board levels. The purpose of school councils, the policy document indicates, is, through the active participation of parents, to improve student achievement and enhance the accountability of the education system to parents. A school council's primary means of achieving its purpose is to make recommendations, in accordance with Ontario Regulation 612/00, to the principal of the school and to the board that established the council. The purpose of PICs is to support, encourage, and enhance parent engagement at the district level to benefit the success of students in achieving a well-rounded and successful education.

The intent of this policy is to ensure that a PIC of a board achieves its purpose by providing information and advice on parent engagement to the board, communicating with and supporting school councils within the board, and undertaking activities to help parents support their children's learning at home and at school.

The following documents provide detailed information on these related policies:

O. Reg. 612/00, "School Councils and Parent Involvement Committees": www.search.e-laws.gov.on.ca/en/search/#Legal Advice

Parents in Partnership: A Parent Engagement Policy for Ontario Schools (2010): www.edu.gov.on.ca/eng/parents/involvement/PE_Policy2010.pdf

The "Parent Engagement Policy page on the Ministry website: www.edu.gov.on.ca/eng/parents/policy.html

It is true that most organizations are currently experiencing cutbacks and dwindling resources—human, physical, and material. They are all re-evaluating the services they provide in an effort to optimize scarce resources and to ensure both efficiency and effectiveness.

One of the roles of principals and other educators is to help broker the services that students need. In these challenging times, when some parents and caregivers are losing their jobs, there is a need to ensure that programs are in place to supplement what homes are not able to provide. Many schools have breakfast, before- and after-school, and recreational programs to assist students. These are particularly important in neighborhoods that are experiencing high levels of poverty and dislocation.

School-to-Work Partnerships

Many school districts have programs designed to assist students in bridging the gaps between school and work. These programs— developed with community members, business, labor, and industry— help students acquire knowledge and experience and develop the skills they need to take hold of opportunities related to the many pathways to college, universities, and the world of work.

Increasingly, business leaders have also become interested in helping to nurture the skills that they will need from future employees. Apprenticeship programs have long been popular in helping to develop marketable skills in students who will go directly to the workplace after high school. The Employability Skills Profile also helps to identify the skills that employers say they wish to see in the graduates of our schools.

Facilitating the Transition to Colleges and Universities

Successful transition to colleges and universities depends on the programs that students have taken in secondary schools and even as early as elementary schools. Course selection should be seen within the K–12 framework. Many programs, including those related to choices, are cumulative in nature, building on the skills that students need to make well-informed decisions.

In Grades 11 and 12, students focus increasingly on individual interests that help them prepare for their postsecondary pathways. In these grades, there are also increased opportunities for learning experiences beyond the school, including co-operative education, work experience, and specialized programs such as the Ontario Youth Apprenticeship Program, Specialist High Skills Major programs, and school-to-work transition programs. These all contribute to the improvement of graduation rates, as they address the interest of students. This, in turn, translates into increased credit accumulation.

School boards are required to ensure that students in Grades 11 and 12 have access to an appropriate destination-related course in at least English, mathematics, and science, in accordance with the course types included in the curriculum policy documents for these disciplines.

The Supervised Alternative Learning (SAL) Example

Section 3.2.3 of *Ontario Schools* (Ontario Ministry of Education, 2011) describes the provincial policy known as Supervised Alternative Learning (SAL). This policy recognizes that most students will attend and success-fully complete secondary school. However, a small number of students are at risk of leaving school early for a wide variety of reasons. The Ministry has many retention and engagement strategies that schools and boards have applied. Nonetheless, if these are not successful, SAL was designed to assist school boards to meet the needs of these students.

The policy states that the goal of SAL is to help ensure that students maintain a connection to learning and to support their continued prog-ress toward graduation or achievement of other educational and per-sonal goals. Ontario Regulation 374/10, "Supervised Alternative Learning and Other Excusals From Attendance at School" (2010), came into effect on February 1, 2011, replacing Regulation 308, "Supervised Alternative Learning for Excused Pupils (SALEP)." The new regulation authorizes the SAL committee of a board to excuse students of compul-sory school age who are at least fourteen years old from attending school while they continue to participate in learning under the supervision of the board or a school of the board. An eligible student may continue in SAL for multiple years, but renewal of the student's program must be authorized by the committee annually.

Key features of SAL under Ontario Regulation 374/10 include the following:

- A SAL plan is required for each student.
- Timelines and procedures are specified for stages in the SAL process.
- A primary contact at the school or board is identified, who will monitor the student's progress at least once per month.
- A transition plan to support the student's transition to his or her next steps after SAL.

A request to participate in the SAL program may be requested by a parent, a student 16 years of age or who has withdrawn from parental control, or a principal. While in SAL, students can participate in a variety of learning activities. These can include taking courses or training, counseling, earning certifications, volunteer or other work, and developing job-search skills and the various essential skills, work habits, and life skills that will help them lead productive adult lives.

It is the responsibility of the principal to ensure that venues off school property have been visited and found appropriate, or are already known and considered appropriate, before the student starts the part of the program that occurs off school property. As much as possible, opportunities to earn credits should be included in the student's program. Some students will eventually graduate or otherwise continue their education as adults.

Part-time study for up to a year is allowed for 16- and 17-year-old students for compassionate reasons, with the principal's approval and without having to go through the SAL process.

These guidelines and implementation strategies may be found in the following documents:

O. Reg. 374/10, "Supervised Alternative Learning and Other Excusals from Attendance at School": www.e-laws.gov.on.ca/ html/regs/english/elaws_regs_100374_e.htm

Supervised Alternative Learning: Policy and Implementation (2010): www.edu.gov.on.ca/eng/policyfunding/SAL2011English.pdf

The main SAL page on the Ministry website: www.edu.gov.on .ca/eng/policyfunding/alternative.html

Creating pathways to graduation requires the collaboration of all community members to bring together the resources to ensure student success. It is clear that schools cannot do this alone. Providing leadership to build alliances to support learning is necessary, as well as partnerships built on trust and communication.

The importance of parental and community engagement in education cannot be overemphasized. It takes many people and groups to ensure that students are fully engaged in the learning process and are successful in school. School–community partnerships bring together educators, parents, and community members to focus on their common purpose—that of student success and high school graduation. Communities today are highly motivated to find ways of overcoming the challenges inherent in partnership development. They also wish to strengthen the alliances necessary for students to feel supported in their quest to receive a high school or equivalent credentials that will help them to pursue other career-related programs.

The Role of Character Development

The implementation of character development helped to create school cultures conducive to learning and to help students develop qualities such as honesty, integrity, fairness, courage, and optimism. The nurturing of these qualities is too important to be left to chance. It becomes necessary for educators to renew their emphasis on preparing students for responsible citizenship in schools and in their communities.

Over 100 years ago, John Dewey (1900) said, "What the best and wisest parent wants for his child, that must the community want for all its children." This points to the importance of all community members ensuring that certain universal values are accessible to all in their desire to take care of the common good. Admittedly, many parents do teach character in their homes. In fact, parents, as a group, are the first character educators. But the fact remains that character development is also a responsibility of educators who are responsible for nurturing all aspects of learning in all domains of education—academic, personal, and interpersonal. When educators place the student at the center of all we do, and when home and school forge partnerships to influence student outcomes intentionally, we create the web of support that is necessary for student success and the continuous improvement of our schools.

Not a New Curriculum, but a Way of Life

Society wants schools to foster positive attributes and to be the embodiment of caring and civility. A systematic character development program nurtures the universal attributes that transcend racial, religious, socioeconomic, cultural, and other lines that divide people in communities and in society at large. To be effective, character education should be a whole-school effort—one that helps to create community and promote the highest ideals of student deportment and citizenship. Character educators agree that these skills and expectations must be nurtured in an explicit, focused, systematic, and intentional manner.

Character education is not a new curriculum; it is a way of life. It is the way we treat others and hold ourselves accountable for ensuring that our actions are compatible with our stated values and beliefs. In implementing the strategies that embed the character attributes into the fabric of the school, all members of the school community seize the "teachable moments" to reinforce the attributes that are identified in co-operation with a wide cross section of community members. Teachers use every opportunity to integrate these attributes into their curriculum and make connections where appropriate. To be effective, these attributes must permeate all policies, programs, practices, and interactions within the school.

As stated consistently by leaders in the field of character education, the development of good character is not inherited but inculcated—it is taught, not caught (Berkowitz, 2007; Lickona, 2004; Vincent, 2004). Students must see what good character looks like and have an opportunity to put it into practice. Popular sayings such as "Children cannot heed a message they have not heard" or "A child is the only substance from which a responsible adult can be made" reflect and reinforce the focus on these programs.

A few years ago, the *Financial Post* carried a series of articles on public views of education. Not surprisingly, parents who saw character development as a primary purpose of schooling rated character education very highly. Studies by Leithwood and Jantzi (2006, 2008), Leithwood and Beatty (2007), and others at the Ontario Institute for Studies in Education also found that, by and large, parents want schools to focus on character education and citizenship development.

A Worldwide Concern

The Character Education Partnership has collected data on the status of character education across the globe. In England, for example, there has been a renewal of commitment to citizenship development. Other countries emphasize character education, describing it as social and emotional learning (United Kingdom); values, ethics, and morals (New South Wales); virtue development and life skills (Lesotho); civic and ethics education (Mexico); value development (Estonia); moral development (Hungary); personal and social development (Malta), to name a few. Countries like Australia indicate, from research conducted in its jurisdiction, that when schools engage in explicit teaching of values, students are more engaged in learning, resulting in improved outcomes.

What we do know is that, increasingly, governments are recognizing that a holistic approach to education includes some form of character development. A common theme that runs throughout these programs is respect for self and others.

As early as the 1990s, we spearheaded initiatives to implement character education in two Ontario district school boards—first, in

York Region (outside Toronto) and, later, in Kawartha Pine Ridge (in Peterborough). Then, in 2008, the Ontario government launched a character development initiative province-wide. Whereas we did not see character development as a panacea, we believed in its possibility to create positive school cultures. We also recognized that it would take all the institutions in our community, working together, for character education to be successful. The saying "It takes a village to raise a child," though perhaps overused, is applicable in this context.

Character Education in Schools

In Ontario, we first implemented character education district-wide in the York Region District School Board. We convened three education forums for a wide cross section of the community, involving some 250 parents, community leaders, and educators. We invited them to reflect on the culture that they wished to foster in York Region schools and the attributes they wanted our schools to emphasize. The forums created a space for a conversation about the role of schools in preparing citizens for the future and enabled us to forge consensus on the attributes we wanted our students to embody as members of their schools and community, and as future citizens. We convinced our community participants that by focusing on our youth during these very challenging times, we were helping to create the future we all wished to have. We emphasized that we would also be nurturing characteristics identified by the business community as integral to the development of a strong work ethic and as prerequisites for success in the workplace.

At the end of the three sessions, the participants decided on ten attributes that they wanted us to develop in our schools. These were respect, responsibility, honesty, integrity, empathy, fairness, initiative, perseverance, courage, and optimism.

Of great interest is the fact that when we conducted a similar exercise in the Kawartha Pine Ridge District School Board, members of that community chose the same ten attributes. The editorial in the local papers suggested that we can, indeed, find common ground on the values that we espouse.

Ontario schools are at different stages in the implementation of this strategy. Many have collected data that demonstrate that when this strategy is implemented in a systematic and intentional manner, there are differences in areas such as suspension, attendance, and other negative behaviors. As well, positive behaviors are evident as students demonstrate the attributes in their day-to-day interactions. The government has collected numerous examples from schools on the impact that character development is having on the culture of schools and on student outcomes.

Building Communities of Character

Elected officials play a pivotal role in the development of a civil society. For this reason, the "building communities of character" phase of the character initiative solicited the support local mayors, politicians, and community leaders. This was an opportunity to establish partnerships to engage the community in an ongoing, systematic, and focused character education effort. The strategy included a wide cross section of the community, including parents and educators as well as members of our business and faith communities, government officials, the police, and labor and social work representatives—these individuals were interested in school improvement and in making the community safe, inclusive, and inviting.

Through our collective efforts, York Region became the first jurisdiction in Canada to develop a character initiative to serve as an example of how community development can be led by the education sector. York Region defines their *character community* as a community committed to keeping and enhancing a place where families are strong, homes and streets are safe, education is effective, businesses are productive, and neighbors care about one another. (For more information on York Region's Character Community Foundation, visit http://www.charactercommunity.com.)

In diverse societies, especially, the need to find common ground on the values that we share becomes a necessity. It is also important for the youth to know what we stand for as a community. After all, they are receiving many messages through movies, television, and other media. How are we helping them to know that respect for self and others is a fundamental value that will help them live with others effectively in a community? How are we teaching them that respect for property and the environment will assist our efforts to sustain our resources? As stated before, these important aspects of education must be taught. They cannot be left to chance.

Character in the Workplace

York Region and Kawartha Pine Ridge may well have been the first school districts in Canada to establish "character in the workplace" initiatives in a systematic and intentional manner. We brought the school district employees together and asked them to consider participating in a program similar to those that were in progress in the district's schools and the wider community. Once introduced, we insisted that the initiative should be led by employees, and asked for volunteers. The initiative was led by a secretary and a member of the business department who was a former janitor and custodian. The strategy introduced staff members to the common purpose of character development and assisted them in modeling and demonstrating the highest standards of character in dealing with their colleagues and with the public. The school board also began to celebrate a character attribute each month and encouraged everyone working for the district to put these tenets into daily practice and to embody them in interpersonal relationships and in customer service. Employees assumed leadership for the ongoing implementation of the initiative. Many volunteered to assist teachers in schools. The employees stated that this strategy had a positive impact on morale and organizational commitment.

There was a strong conviction that the character development initiative would make a difference in the culture of the organization and in the service quality that was provided to students, parents, and the community. The district's next step was to take this initiative to the business community. In this community, as well, there was a call for volunteers to support teachers in schools. The notion that schools cannot educate children alone was widely communicated within the community. There was a surge of support for the district as parents and grandparents volunteered as tutors in the schools. College and university students were paid to support their local schools through the "Tutors in the Classroom" program we initiated.

Citizenship Development

Canada, as other nations around the world, is part of a governing process that attempts to serve the best interests of society. Citizenship is a right as well as a very important responsibility. With citizenship come rights such as freedom of expression, religion, and lifestyle. However, these rights come with expectations such as the responsibility all share to support the democratic process within the nation. These responsibilities are manifested in many ways. Citizens are expected to work hard to maintain and improve the economic, political, and social aspects of the society. Citizenship is a right, but it is more importantly a privilege that cannot be taken for granted.

In Ontario, for example, through mandatory courses in civics and history, as well as optional courses in law and world issues, the public education system has introduced students to the ideals of a democratic society and fostered pro-social concepts of citizenship among the younger generation. The Ministry of Education also requires mandatory community service for students prior to graduation to encourage community involvement and responsibility and to promote civic engagement.

It is important, in a world dominated by popular culture in which very confusing messages reach our young people every day, to reinforce the need for an active and involved citizenry. We need to teach these important elements of democracy in a manner that engages young minds and harness their enthusiasm, optimism, and desire to help others. Voting, for example, is one way to demonstrate responsible citizenship. And with reports of fewer and fewer people taking the time to participate in civic pursuits such as voting in elections, the need to revitalize interest in citizenship development remains an important aspect of schooling.

Young people are willing to take on these responsibilities. Many fully realize the need to create a world where citizenship and all its privileges, rights, and responsibilities are extended to all. Schools can play a pivotal role in modeling what good citizenship looks like and in nurturing the behaviors, attitudes, and dispositions that sustain positive relationships and create civility and responsibility.

Implementing character development has helped us to create community in Ontario schools and school districts. The inclusive nature of the initiative brought people together, contributed to social cohesion, and helped community members find common ground. After one of the consultation sessions, one parent said, "You have put the public back into public education."

The business community also depends on the school system to help develop the graduates who will ultimately work in their companies and institutions. Business leaders often say that they can develop the technical skills, but they want schools to develop qualities such as initiative, perseverance, and honesty.

There is definitely a need for schools to play their role in developing qualities such as empathy and respect, to take seriously the intent of holistic education to educate hearts as well as minds. It has become a priority for educators to ensure that the core value of preparing students to think critically, feel deeply and empathetically, and act wisely and ethically is critical today. With rapid scientific advancements, it is important that high school graduates be equipped to make ethical decisions and to contribute to the well-being of others within their communities.

Asking Ourselves Some Tough Questions

Reflection contributes to learning and improvement. It was necessary for us to ask tough questions about our own commitment to ensuring that schools contribute to positive outcomes for all students, especially those from diverse populations and those who live in poverty. These questions may serve as a means of self-reflection for others who are working at school improvement:

- ✓ Are we truly committed to achieving both excellence and equity?
- ✓ How are we ensuring that poverty does not determine destiny?
- ✓ What are we doing to help individual teachers move to the next level of expertise and confidence?
- ✓ How are we using evidence/data to propel change in individual student performance?
- ✓ Are we intervening early to provide the necessary supports for students who are falling behind?
- ✓ Is providing meaningful feedback to students and adults an essential component of the improvement strategy?
- ✓ What is the agenda when district leaders visit schools? Is the monitoring of progress toward stated goals an objective?
- ✓ How are we assisting principals in creating the conditions for student learning?
- ✓ What are we doing to embed a sense of shared accountability for student achievement in schools?
- ✓ How can we best personalize and customize learning?
- ✓ Do we know how minoritized groups and other subpopulations, such as boys, are achieving in our schools? Have we disaggregated our data to have a clear picture of how each group is performing?
- ✓ What are we doing to foster the notion of schools as networks to build lateral capacity?
- ✓ Have we considered pairing high- and low-performing schools to facilitate the sharing of promising practices?
- ✓ What are we doing to create a culture of inquiry and experimentation?
- ✓ How do we ensure the consistent implementation of high-impact strategies in all schools?
- ✓ What are we doing to embed some key components of successful leadership for school improvement? For example,

  - ✓ Developing a laser-like focus on achievement
  - ✓ Creating a culture of high expectations for learning

✓ Ensuring rigor, relevance, positive relationships

✓ Focusing on enhancing professional accountability

✓ Maintaining a sense of urgency to improve graduation rates

✓ Are we truly committed to ensuring meaningful parental and community involvement?

✓ Are we providing the outreach necessary to bring other partners, such as the business community, to the table?

✓ What intervention strategies will we use to assist students who are at the risk of dropping out of school?

✓ How will we deepen the conversation to assume an even greater sense of responsibility for the role of schools in improving student achievement?

Future Directions

The province of Ontario has seen steady improvement in student achievement. In a spirit of continuous improvement, educators are sharpening the focus in areas such as critical thinking, creativity, and higher-order skills. The need to improve problem-solving and knowledge application is a priority. Future directions also include moving from the mastery of facts to an understanding of "big ideas," using more interdisciplinary approaches. There is an even more intense focus on collaborative inquiry into problems of practice and on other enabling factors such as the implementation of a comprehensive early learning and childcare system.

Educators today are strategically placed to achieve both excellence and equity, to focus on results, and to close the seemingly intractable achievement gaps. At this time in our development as a professional community, we need a new conversation about the role of schools and schooling. Variations in learning, for example, should no longer be attributed to background factors. Schools should persist in assuming even greater responsibility to remove barriers, engage students, and create the conditions necessary to ensure that more students graduate from high schools. Increasingly, schools must be builders of a civic society and advocates for students who are poor or disadvantaged in any way. School leaders must create the conditions for parents to participate fully in their children's education and, at the same time, ensure that their school's primary focus is to serve the needs of students. They must be architects of change, creating a legacy of developing global citizens and solution finders—individuals who have a strong commitment to improving the lives of others at home and abroad. Admittedly, there is no shortage of schools that are already engaged in these pursuits.

High School Graduation represents a continuum of developmentally appropriate ideas and strategies that contribute to student achievement. There is proof that these strategies contribute to improvement in student learning. In Ontario, for example, graduation rates have improved significantly, with over 93,000 more students graduating from high school. This did not happen by chance; it is the result of a sound strategy, with a focus on capacity building, and a nonpunitive, talent-releasing approach to education reform. This strategy eschewed the shame-and-blame, one-size-fits-all approach; instead, it was based on respect for the profession and validation of the pivotal role that educators play in improving school systems.

Ultimately, the success of the Ontario education system—and, indeed, other systems across the world—rests on the quality of our graduates—their knowledge, skills, values, and willingness to make a difference in the lives of others. Society depends on this rich resource of human capital that is nurtured in our schools. Early and ongoing success, from kindergarten to graduation, remains a societal necessity and educational responsibility.

References

Berkowitz, M. (2007). *A brief history of character education in the U.S.: 1954–2004.* Unpublished manuscript.

Dewey, J. (1900). *The school and society: Being three lectures.* Chicago: University of Chicago Press.

Drucker, P. (1999). The new pluralism. In F. Hesselbein, M. Goldsmith, & I. Somervilled (Eds.), *Leading beyond the walls: How high-performing organizations collaborate for shared success* (pp. 9–18). San Francisco: Jossey-Bass.

Edelstein, H. (in press). *Developing collaborative research partnerships for knowledge mobilization.* University of Toronto, Doctoral dissertation in preparation.

Epstein, J. L. (2001). *School, family, and community partnerships: Preparing educators and improving schools.* Boulder, CO: Westview Press.

Israel, B. A., Schulz, A. J., Parker, E. A., & Becker, A. B. (1998). Review of community-based research: Assessing partnership approaches to improve public health. *Annual Review of Public Health, 19*(1), 173–202.

Lasker, R., & Weiss, E. (2003). Broadening participation in community problem solving: A multidisciplinary model to support collaborative research. *Journal of Urban Health, 80*(1), 14–47.

Leithwood, K., & Beatty, B. (2007). *Leading with teacher emotions in mind.* Thousand Oaks, CA: Corwin.

Leithwood, K., & Jantzi, D. (2006). *A critical review of the parent engagement literature.* Toronto: Ontario Ministry of Education.

Leithwood, K., & Jantzi, D. (2008). Linking leadership to student learning: The role of collective efficacy. *Educational Administration Quarterly, 44*(4), 496–528.

Lickona, T. (2004) *Character matters: How to help our children develop good judgment, integrity, and other essential virtues.* New York: Touchstone.

Ontario Ministry of Education. (2008). *Finding common ground: Character development in Ontario Schools, K–12.* Toronto: Queens Printer for Ontario.

Ontario Ministry of Education. (2010). *Parents in partnership: A parent engagement policy for Ontario schools.* Toronto: Queens Printer for Ontario.

Ontario Ministry of Education. (2011). *Ontario schools, Kindergarten to Grade 12, policy and program requirements, 2011.* Toronto: Queens Printer for Ontario. Retrieved from http://www.edu.gov.on.ca/eng/document/policy/os/ONSchools.pdf

Ross, P. (1994). *Parent involvement and learning.* Unpublished manuscript.

Sergiovanni, T. (1994). *Building community in schools.* San Francisco. Jossey-Bass.

Vincent, P. F. (2004*). Developing character in students: A workbook for teachers, parents, and communities.* Chapel Hill, NC: Character Development Group.

York Region. (2002, January 24). *Character community update and resolution* (Report No. 1 of the regional chief administrative officer). Newmarket, ON: Regional Municipality of York. Retrieved from http://www.york.ca/NR/rdonlyres/x5pdxstrcxucaeoycvsom2dwchddn6xhrubtwcyucmrwag4ad6c4oijdsb4x6otqokeldlky372zknsvu5xlmrhb7c/rpt1.pdf

Appendices

APPENDIX 1

SMART Goals

Specific and Strategic

Questions to Ask	Observations/ Evidence	Comments/ Recommendations
Have you articulated precisely what you want to achieve?		
Have priorities been strategically selected based on an analysis of system or school data?		
Is the goal aligned to specific curriculum expectations?		
Does the goal represent the greatest area of need for students?		
In what area(s) are a significant number of students experiencing difficulty?		

Measurable

Has a baseline been established?		
What tools will best measure if targets have been achieved?		
How often will you measure progress?		
What is the achievement target for the school?		
How will you know if you have been successful in achieving your goal?		

Attainable/Achievable

Is what you are expecting reasonable? How do you know?		
Is the goal ambitious yet attainable?		
How can you build capacity to achieve the desirable change? How do you get buy-in from everyone to ensure you achieve your priorities?		

Results Oriented

What will be different for students if you achieve your goal?		
Why is it important to achieve this goal? For students? For staff?		
How will you monitor your progress?		
Have you clearly articulated your desired results?		
How will you communicate your progress?		

Time Bound

What is the time frame for achieving this goal?		
What strategies are in place to keep you on track? (Monitoring strategies at specific points in time are identified.)		

APPENDIX 2

District or School Improvement Plan

Needs Assessment

Members of the Improvement Team

Achievement and Other Relevant Data

Areas of Strength

Successful Practices

Areas of Concern

Based on these data, where should we focus our efforts? What are our SMART goals?

Smart Goal 1:

Strategies	Resources Required	Professional Learning Required	Leadership Development	Parental Engagement	Monitoring		Measures of Progress	Status
					Timelines	Responsibility		

Smart Goal 2:

Strategies	Resources Required	Professional Learning Required	Leadership Development	Parental Engagement	Monitoring		Measures of Progress	Status
					Timelines	Responsibility		

Smart Goal 3:

Strategies	Resources Required	Professional Learning Required	Leadership Development	Parental Engagement	Monitoring		Measures of Progress	Status
					Timelines	Responsibility		

APPENDIX 3

Key Questions to Support Improvement Planning

Needs Assessment

> Where are we now? Where do we want to be?

- What do our student achievement data tell us?
- Have we disaggregated the data to identify groups of students who are not meeting with success?
- Are there differences in achievement among similar schools or populations?
- What trends or patterns in student achievement do we see that we are trying to support or alter?
- Have we carefully examined the data to identify underlying causes of strengths and weaknesses in achievement?
- What improvement targets have we set?

Identifying Goals

> What should we focus on?

- Based on our diagnosis and data, what will we focus on to raise student achievement?
- What are the three or four priorities that we will focus on to ensure student success? What barriers must be overcome?
- Will these priorities address both short-term needs and actions and long-term sustainable improvement?
- What will we do to achieve equity of outcomes?

The Plan

What will we do?

- What are the specific strategies and actions that we will implement to achieve our priorities?
- How will the district engage and support schools and communities in this process?
- Does the plan identify the roles, responsibilities, time frame, and resources to support implementation strategies?
- How will we provide required professional learning and capacity building?
- Have we drawn on research and professional experience to select the best strategies to maximize student learning?
- Are all strategies in the plan clear, concise, and consistent with the key priorities? Are they integrated and mutually supportive?
- How will we communicate the plan to our schools and communities?

Action, Monitoring, and Evaluation

Is our plan making a difference? How do we know?

- How will we communicate our actions and results?
- How will we measure our progress and the impact on student learning?
- How has instructional practice changed?
- How will we address changing needs or issues that may be identified in the monitoring and review process?
- How will our diagnostic and monitoring information support future improvement planning?

APPENDIX 4

Sample Improvement Plan Checklist

District Target Setting and Improvement Planning: Key Components

District _____

		Comment
	• The district improvement team is in place, with roles and responsibilities defined.	
	• Priorities are determined through analysis of district data.	
	• There is a clear focus.	
	• A limited number of goals is clearly articulated based on data analysis and determination of the greatest areas of student need.	
	• Indicators of success are measurable in terms of student achievement.	
	• Required resources are identified. • The district's budget priorities align with achievement priorities.	
	• Clear timelines are articulated.	
	• District targets are established. • Specific strategies to achieve goals and meet targets are identified.	
	• Accountability systems are established: Who is responsible? How will progress be monitored? How often?	
	• Equity issues are being addressed (e.g., low-performing schools, struggling students, strategies are in place to support specific subpopulations).	
	• Capacity-building strategies are in place to support the implementation of the plan (e.g., learning communities, job-embedded professional learning, leadership development).	

(Continued)

(Continued)

		Comment
	• Are there expectations that school plans align with district plans?	
	• Communication strategies are in place to ensure everyone understands the plan and knows their role. • Strategies to engage the community are identified.	
	• At what point will targets, strategies, responsibilities, and resources be revised or adapted?	
	• Has there been an evaluation of the previous year's plan? Were the commitments in the previous plan achieved? • If not, why? What were the obstacles? Are there strategies in place to overcome the obstacles?	

APPENDIX 5

School Target Setting and Improvement Planning: Key Components

School _____

		Comment
	• A school improvement team is in place, with roles and responsibilities defined.	
	• A needs assessment has been conducted to determine school improvement priorities.	
	• A small number of precise improvement goals is identified.	
	• Ambitious school achievement targets are established.	
	• Specific strategies to achieve goals and targets are identified.	
	• Measurable indicators of success are in place.	
	• Required resources are identified.	
	• Clear timelines are articulated.	
	• Monitoring systems have been established: Who is responsible? How will progress be monitored, and how often? At what point will targets, strategies, responsibilities, and resources be revised or adapted?	
	• Equity issues are being addressed (e.g., struggling students, strategies are in place to support specific subpopulations) through differentiated instruction.	
	• Capacity-building strategies are in place to support the implementation of the plan.	
	• Communication strategies are in place to ensure that individuals understand the plan and know their roles.	
	• There are strategies in place to engage parents and the community.	
	• How have you planned, if needed, for mid-course corrections in the plan?	
	• Has there been an evaluation of the previous year's plan? Were commitments in the previous plan achieved? • If not, why? What were the obstacles? Are there strategies in place to overcome the obstacles?	

Index

CORWIN

A SAGE Company

The Corwin logo—a raven striding across an open book—represents the union of courage and learning. Corwin is committed to improving education for all learners by publishing books and other professional development resources for those serving the field of PreK–12 education. By providing practical, hands-on materials, Corwin continues to carry out the promise of its motto: **"Helping Educators Do Their Work Better."**

ONTARIO PRINCIPALS' COUNCIL

Exemplary Leadership in Public Education

The Ontario Principals' Council (OPC) is a voluntary association for principals and vice-principals in Ontario's public school system. We believe that exemplary leadership results in outstanding schools and improved student achievement. To this end, we foster quality leadership through world-class professional services and supports. As an ISO 9001 registered organization, we are committed to **"quality leadership—our principal product."**